CASH

The 4 Keys to Better Sales, Smarter Marketing,
and a Supercharged Revenue Machine

A. LEE JUDGE

For *Salespeople* Who Need to Understand *Marketing*.
For *Marketers* Who Need to Understand *Sales*.

CASH

OMMUNICATION · ALIGNMENT · SYSTEMS · HONESTY

The 4 Keys to Better Sales, Smarter Marketing, and a Supercharged Revenue Machine

A. LEE JUDGE

ISBN: 979-8-9911630-2-6

TILT
PUBLISHING

Tilt Publishing
700 Park Offices Drive, Suite 250
Research Triangle, NC 27709

Dedication

This book is dedicated to my parents. To my father, Alexander Lee Judge, Sr., who, through his business endeavors, taught me how to develop a business, love working with a diversity of people, and understand the concept of matching customer needs to a service solution. To my mother, Rebecca H. Judge, who taught me the power of clear communication and professionalism under pressure and that it's never too late to start or learn something new. Thank you both for building my self-confidence and desire to help others be their best.

Also, to my sisters, Brenda, Beverly, and Sheila, who provided examples of hard work, creativity, and determination. I can't imagine where I would be, or who I would have become, without your love and support.

Acknowledgments

I want to extend my gratitude to all the amazing individuals who have positively influenced my journey in Sales and Marketing. To the incredible leaders, colleagues, and mentors who have guided, challenged, and inspired me along the way: your wisdom and support have been invaluable.

A special thanks to:

Lee and Larry Camp, Giddy Hollander, Guy Yair, Chris du Toit, Kumaran Shanmuhan, Clay Davis, Cary Hargett, Brandon Yohn, Lawrence Dixon, David Ellis, Morris Finley, Cedric Maddox, Terry McLane, Carlester Crumpler, and my Pastor, Lee Allen Jenkins.

To those who took the time to share their expertise and experience with me so I could share it with you: Matt Crisp, Todd Ervin, Pam Didner, Joe Pulizzi, Mark Schaefer, Laura Erdem, Aaron Hassen, Sandy Carter, Seth Godin, and Darrell Alfonso.

I thank the team members at Content Monsta who helped coordinate interviews and provided me the time needed to write this book: Alaina Case, Marc Raco, and my wife, Laura Judge.

Alex and Zion—thank you for closing my office door when you saw Daddy writing. I appreciate you and love you both from A to Z.

Table of Contents

Part 3

SYSTEMS

Part 4

HONESTY

For ongoing engagement and community conversations around this book and topic, please visit:

ALeeJudge.com/cash

where you can:

- Connect with the author and experts featured in the book.
- Learn about innovations in the fields of Sales and Marketing.

Use this QR Code to listen to the full conversations with featured experts, hear the *CASH Book Podcast,* and obtain other supplemental content related to the book.

Connect and follow A. Lee Judge on all relevant social networks:

- Linkedin.com/in/aleejudge
- Instagram.com/@ALeeJudge
- Tiktok.com/@a.leejudge
- Facebook.com/ALeeJudgeOfficial

Discover how well your organization is harnessing the power of your Sales and Marketing teams to build a true revenue machine. Take this quick assessment and see where you stand.

TaketheCASHtest.com

Introduction

This book is designed for three specific types of people: those who aspire to excel in Sales, those who are driven to succeed in Marketing, and those who aim to merge these disciplines to enhance business revenue. After reading this book, you will possess a profound understanding of the intersection between Sales and Marketing and you will be equipped to propel your career and business to greater heights through the unification of these two critical teams.

The CASH framework is your four-key road map to success. It begins with mastering *communication*, which ensures that Sales and Marketing work in sync rather than in silos. Next, *alignment* focuses both teams on shared goals, fostering a unified approach to achieving business outcomes. By implementing effective *systems*, you'll streamline processes and create a solid foundation that supports consistent, scalable growth. Finally, upholding *honesty* builds the trust and transparency essential for long-term success. Each key is crucial, and understanding how to leverage each of them will equip you to drive both your career and business forward.

Success in Sales now requires a solid grasp of marketing principles, while success in Marketing equally demands an understanding of sales tactics. Whether you are a Sales professional keen to master marketing strategies or a Marketing professional eager to comprehend sales strategies, this book will empower you to excel in your role and profession. Leaders will find this resource invaluable for integrating Sales and Marketing into a cohesive, high-performing Revenue team.

When I embarked on writing this book, I sought the simplest way to delineate the roles of Sales and Marketing. Initially, I defined them as follows:

> **Sales** persuades people to *buy things*, whether they want them or not.
>
> **Marketing** makes people *desire things*, whether they need them or not.

Although accurate, these definitions too often emphasize the separate goals of each team, leading to potential conflicts. By the end of your journey through this book, you will adopt a more holistic definition that aligns Sales and Marketing not only with the company's objectives but also with the needs of the customer.

Our ultimate goal is to transcend the traditional separation of Sales and Marketing teams by fostering a unified Revenue Team. Such a team collaborates seamlessly to generate profitable business and cultivate loyal customers. This book guides Sales and Marketing professionals to understand and leverage each other's roles effectively, functioning together as a singular, formidable revenue generation entity. It also serves as a practical resource for teams that struggle with collaboration, offering strategies to bridge these divides.

The book's structure caters to your needs in two distinct ways. For a thorough understanding of how Sales and Marketing can work as one, read it from cover to cover. Here you'll discover comprehensive insights into how these areas can collaborate effectively. Alternatively, if you specialize in Sales or Marketing, feel free to dive into the sections most relevant to your role. Each segment is crafted to stand alone and provide practical advice and real-world examples that you can apply immediately in your daily activities.

In addition to my insights and experiences, you'll benefit from contributions by other executives, experts, and practitioners whose credible experiences have been incorporated following the book's initial manuscript completion. These perspectives offer unique insights and real-world scenarios that enrich the lessons contained within these pages.

As you progress through this book, you will identify areas within your company that require enhancement. Not only will this book equip you with the knowledge to become a more effective Sales or Marketing professional; it will also provide you with the keys to creating an efficient revenue machine through the cohesion of Sales and Marketing.

Origin Story

My journey to understanding the solutions to this collaboration challenge began on the first day of a new job at a software company. The state of the company was one in which the Marketing team had slowly dwindled away and the Salespeople were performing more like independent agents rather than members of a cohesive team. Chris, the last marketer to exit, interviewed me on his way out of the door. I didn't know he was leaving until my first day on the job. That's when I was shown my new office—his old one.

Emily, the kind and soft-spoken lady from HR, came by to give me an office tour. We walked down the hallway where most of the Sales team had offices. Many were empty, but it was early in the day, so I assumed most of the employees had not arrived yet.

Halfway down the hallway, she abruptly turned around and headed back in the direction that we had come from. I asked, "Who's offices are down there?"

"No one now," she replied.

I sensed there was a lot more to that story. However, I also sensed that it wasn't something she wanted to (or should) talk about with a new employee.

Things became more apparent when Giddy, the CEO, visited my office later that day. It turns out that the Marketing team was gone, and I was the new marketing employee number one. I learned that Giddy had recently returned to the company out of retirement and was there to get the company back on track. For the moment, he was serving multiple roles as CEO, CMO, and VP of Sales.

Giddy also interviewed me the same day that Chris did. During the interview, I explained to Giddy that I had programmed multiple customer database systems for my earlier employer. At that time, I didn't know what a CRM was (or that the letters stood for customer relationship management), even though I had built at least six relational databases for customer data and reporting. I had avoided applying for jobs that said "Salesforce experience preferred" because it sounded foreign to me. I didn't know that I knew a programming language—even though I had hand-coded most of the databases using SQL in the backend of Microsoft Access. Giddy knew exactly what I was capable of, even if I didn't.

By the second week, Giddy came into my office and said, "I want you to be the administrator for our Salesforce instance." Despite my avoiding this *CRM thing*, Giddy had just dumped that monster in my lap. He followed up by telling me that he also wanted me to make sure the Sales users became more religious about actually using Salesforce so he could get a better grasp of sales activities. I officially became a Salesforce administrator, thrown in headfirst.

A few weeks later, Chris returned to the company and raised the Marketing team back to a team of two. We worked closely together for the next seven years, pulling together Sales and Marketing. I am grateful to him for his knowledge and expertise, which have helped me through this journey. I faced many challenges and learned immensely, so if you're reading this, Chris, thanks for coming back. This story wouldn't exist without you.

And so it begins. I'm a marketer in charge of the Sales CRM and tasked with rejuvenating a Sales team's data, processes, reporting, and collaboration with Marketing. I faced all the common challenges that most organizations face between Sales and Marketing. And after working through all these challenges, I've learned they can all be solved by the CASH keys that we will discuss in this book.

My career constantly placed me in the middle of the road between Sales teams and Marketing teams. This led to a unique perspective into their pains and desires. It forced me to understand the big picture of a business organization above the silos of Sales and Marketing. It taught me to speak the language of both Sales and Marketing.

These experiences created tense moments, however. Including one that found me sitting in a boardroom, hand raised—about to question the validity of a Sales member's claim.

That pivotal moment revealed the four critical keys taught in this book. It exposed signs that the two teams had not been communicating sufficiently and weren't aligned in their strategies. Luckily there were systems in place to unveil the truth and keep us honest. We'll come back to this story later.

Part 1

Communication

Communication between Sales and Marketing is crucial for a successful partnership. It involves intentional exchanges of information and a cooperative relationship. At their best, these two seemingly independent entities operate in unison, understanding each other's movements.

In the next few chapters we explore the nuances of Sales and Marketing communication. We will discuss the patterns that shape this interaction and how they can influence business goals. Whether it's sharing digital insights about prospects or the flow of information about closed deals, the key is establishing a strategically closed communication loop.

Sales and Marketing need to do more than just talk to each other. They must truly listen, understand, and respond. This is the gateway to a seamless and successful partnership.

Chapter 1

Who's in the Meeting?
The Importance of Presence

A great place to start the discussion about Sales and Marketing communication is talking about our meetings. Yes, those often-dreaded gatherings that fill our calendars. Meetings can sometimes feel like they're consuming our workdays. But here's an interesting thought—what if these meetings were the way to unlock more effective collaboration between our Sales and Marketing teams?

You see, the Sales team and the Marketing team often operate in their own silos. They plan their strategies, discuss their goals, and tackle their challenges independently. However, this siloed approach can lead to a lack of shared understanding and, consequently, a lack of real collaboration.

So, how do we break down these silos? Where's the perfect starting point for nurturing this collaboration? The answer might be more straightforward than we think. It starts with opening the doors of our meeting rooms. Figure 1.1 captures the essence of the problem.

Attending each other's meetings offers a golden opportunity for Sales and Marketing to get firsthand insight into the other team's world. For the Sales team, it's a chance to understand the creative process and see the research, effort, and thought that goes into each marketing campaign. For the Marketing team, it's an opportunity to learn about customer interactions, to hear the objections, and to comprehend the challenges faced by Sales.

Bridging this gap doesn't mean every meeting needs to become a full house. It's about inviting primary members from each team to pertinent meetings where they can offer valuable insights, ask relevant questions, and perhaps, most importantly, listen and understand.

Let's remember: True collaboration begins with understanding. And what better way to understand than to witness the processes, the planning, and the problem-solving as they happen? By stepping into each other's meeting rooms, we step into each other's shoes, creating a foundation of empathy and mutual respect—the perfect breeding ground for collaboration.

Let me share a story with you that illustrates the power of this simple yet game-changing action.

After several years working between Marketing and Sales, many of the Sales team members began to recognize the value of Marketing's data. Oren, the VP of Sales, was particularly tuned in to the value of working closely with Marketing—from a lead generation standpoint and also for understanding the data behind the company's customer journey.

One day, Oren made sure that I attended a particular sales meeting. It was a budget review, and the Sales team members found themselves defending the trade shows where they wanted to exhibit for the year. The CEO was out to cut most as he hadn't seen much return on recent trade show investments. Oren had worked closely with the Marketing team throughout the year and was prepared to defend his event.

The first salesperson spoke up to defend his favorite trade show. The best he could show to prove the ROI for the event was that he conducted several potential client meetings during the event. Because he wasn't in tune with marketing activities, he couldn't speak about where those leads originated or where they currently were in the pipeline. He only knew that he hadn't closed a deal in connection with those event meetings. His show was cut.

The second salesperson didn't fare much better. He could show all the people he scanned at his last event; however, he couldn't confirm if they were already in the pipeline, had met at the event, or had interacted with the company since. His show was cut too.

Next was Oren. His event was the costliest of all the events on the chopping block. However, he handled his show very differently. Months before the show, Oren and I worked to determine who of his prospects were most likely to go to the show. With Marketing's help, he created nurture campaigns to develop a relationship that led to warm meetings with potential clients at the event.

In addition to the meetings at the event, Oren and Marketing planned a quick follow-up method for anyone that was scanned at the trade show booth. They were automatically assigned to Oren in the CRM and received a personal letter from him. By the time Oren and his prospects had returned to their respective offices after the event, the prospects had left a clear trail of engagement with Oren and the company.

It didn't stop there. The data trail flowed into all the opportunities created by Oren in the CRM from these prospects. The data showed that the company's biggest deal that year had followed a clear path through the trade show funnel we designed, from an unknown lead to a closed deal.

Oren kept and attended that show again the following year. Budget approved.

Marketers in Sales Meetings

In some organizations, getting a marketing seat at the table can be a challenge. Marketers tend to get shut out of the Sales team's meetings until creativity or a top-of-the-funnel report is needed. This is even more prevalent in organizations that see Marketing as the "art and events" department. I gained access to sales meetings such as the one with Oren by continually showing the added value that I, as a marketer, brought to sales meetings.

Gaining access to sales meetings as a marketer can significantly enhance your understanding of the sales process and improve cohesion between both teams. If your organization doesn't typically include marketers in sales meetings, here are some strategies you could employ to get involved:

> **Express Interest:** This may sound simple, but letting Sales know that you are interested in understanding their process and challenges better could open the door. Expressing a genuine interest in their work can show that you are available to assist in their strategies and are also interested in learning how to make your marketing efforts more effective for them.

> **Propose a Cross-Functional Meeting:** If going directly into a sales meeting seems like a big step initially, propose a cross-functional meeting where members from both teams can share insights, plans, and challenges. This meeting can serve as

an open forum that encourages communication and cooperation between the two teams.

Request a Shadowing Opportunity: If it's possible, ask to shadow a salesperson for a day or during a few calls. This hands-on experience can give you valuable insight into the sales process and open the door for you to be included in future sales meetings.

Offer Value: If you can demonstrate that your presence in the meetings will add value, the Sales team is more likely to welcome your participation. Perhaps you can offer marketing insights that can help the Sales team better understand customer behavior, industry trends, or competitors.

Find an Advocate: If there's someone from the Sales team who understands the importance of alignment with Marketing, enlist their support. They can help you convey the value of having Marketing involved in Sales' meetings.

Promote Sales and Marketing Alignment: Continually promote the idea that better alignment between Sales and Marketing can lead to increased revenue. Use data and case studies to make your case. If the leadership understands the tangible benefits of this alignment, they are more likely to support your participation in sales meetings.

Remember, the ultimate goal here is not just to get an invite to the meetings, but to foster a culture of cooperation and mutual respect between Sales and Marketing. That's where the real value lies.

Salespeople in Marketing Meetings

From a salesperson's point of view, there may not seem to be any value in attending a marketing meeting and convincing the Sales team to attend can be a bit of a challenge. It's not just a question of granting them access but, more importantly, making them understand the immense value these meetings can bring to their work.

When speaking to Sales teams or their leadership, use these compelling reasons regarding why investing their time in marketing meetings could be one of the best decisions they make:

Understanding the Big Picture: Marketing strategies are built around long-term goals and overall business objectives. Being part of these meetings helps Sales to understand this broader perspective, providing valuable context that can enhance your approach to selling and customer relationships. Marketing's understanding of the long game can be foreign to salespeople who have to hit quarterly numbers. Sharing the big picture can help a salesperson translate long-term strategy into repeatable end-of-quarter results.

Gaining Insight into Customer Personas: Marketers dedicate significant effort to researching and creating detailed customer personas. These personas, which represent your target customers, are a goldmine of information about customer needs, pain points, and buying behaviors that could be invaluable in shaping your sales tactics. Marketing teams should have research on demographics (age, gender, income, etc.) and psychographics (attitudes, values, goals)—both containing valuable insights into customers that Sales needs in order to have the most effective outreach.

Gaining Product Knowledge: In well-structured organizations, Marketing teams are heavily involved in product development processes and consequently have a deep understanding of the products or services being sold. They can provide insights about unique selling points, competitive advantages, and potential applications that you might not be aware of. This can significantly improve your product pitching and demonstration abilities.

Encouraging Shared Responsibility: When you attend marketing meetings, you're sending a powerful message that you view success as a shared responsibility. This enhances cross-functional camaraderie, fostering an atmosphere where departments are more willing to help each other out. And when Marketing is more informed about the realities of selling, they can create better materials, resources, and strategies that directly address your needs.

Getting Early Warnings on Campaigns: Attending marketing meetings gives you a heads-up on upcoming marketing campaigns. This allows you to prepare in advance and align your strategies to leverage these campaigns for maximum impact. It also gives salespeople a chance to raise any red flags from the field (customer interactions) that Marketing may not be aware of.

To sum it up, taking the time to attend marketing meetings is a strategic move that can lead to better-informed and more effective sales strategies. As the front-liners in revenue generation, having a holistic view of the organization's efforts can only enhance your capabilities, helping you close deals more effectively and consistently.

Expert Insight—Pam Didner

Pam Didner is a leading consultant in bringing Sales and Marketing teams together. I've attended her workshops and speaking engagements and have extreme respect for her experience in B2B marketing, bridging the gap between technology and marketing, and boosting alignment between Sales and Marketing. In a conversation with Pam, I asked her about what prompted the change regarding the needs of Marketing and Sales to work more closely together. This is what she shared:

Now everything is connected because it's digital. What you do on the phone, you leave a digital footprint. And in terms of what you read, what you consume, what you search, people can actually see what you do. As long as you are online, everything is trackable to some extent. Because of that, because everything is connected nowadays, that means the customer journey from beginning to end is somehow intertwined. So for a long time—marketing was Marketing, sales was Sales, and they didn't really have to talk to each other. Things were fine. Deals were being closed; events were being attended; everything was great.

But now everything is connected . . . and Sales and Marketing still don't talk to each other. From the outside looking in, the customer is going to feel that this joint effort is disconnected. People can see it. So, the talking and communication becomes super-important. However, not many organizations realize it. And even though some realize it, they are not necessarily making an effort to make that connection or build that communication.

Why? Because the revenue didn't suffer that much. If the revenue is not suffering that much, why rock the boat? But if the revenue starts suffering, people will start saying, "We need to do something different!" Then it will force the two to work together, and we see a lot of that now. That's because Sales has a much harder time closing the deal, and then Marketing also gets lesser performance in terms of paid ads and email click-through rates, and also getting the quality of leads. So both sides are feeling the pain, and you are seeing more and more conversation now than ever before.

Chapter 2

Sales-to-Marketing Communication

The real-world dynamics of Sales and Marketing teams often operate in their own parallel lines, creating the silos that we so often refer to. However, one of the most productive ways to increase marketing effectiveness is through an exchange of insights between these teams. Because you as a reader are more likely to read from the perspective of one team or the other, I will address the communication needed from one perspective at a time before we bring it all together.

Listening—the Salesperson's Superpower

In the heart of every thriving business, Sales teams engage directly with prospects. They field questions, counter objections, and listen attentively to the language and expressions that prospects use to articulate their needs, pain points, and aspirations. It's this front-line experience that equips Sales teams with valuable insights—how the prospects describe their world and the words they use to express their needs, pains, and desires.

Now imagine harnessing the Sales team's experiences and insights within your Marketing team's strategies. By sharing this "prospect language" and the common pain points with the Marketing team, Sales can help Marketing tailor content to reflect the customer's voice more accurately.

It's about taking the raw, unfiltered information from the field and translating it into targeted, meaningful, and effective marketing campaigns.

This takes us beyond attracting leads; it allows us to begin fostering a relationship with those leads. When prospects see their pains, needs, and interests reflected in your content, they feel understood. You're creating a connection that builds trust. It demonstrates that your business not only listens but empathizes and seeks to provide the best solution. This is lead nurturing.

As you're beginning to see, this trust starts with Sales being the ears of the organization. Sales, with their direct contact with prospects and customers, are the first to get a sense of shifts in customer needs, emerging trends, and changing market dynamics. Insights on these shifts can help the people in Marketing remain agile, allowing them to adapt their strategies, remain relevant to the target audience, and deliver content to support continued trust building.

As I mentioned earlier, you can initiate this flow of communication by simply joining each other's meetings. It is crucial to establish a regular channel for Sales to share their insights with Marketing. Beyond regular meeting discussions, you can establish a communication base through a shared digital platform such as a CMS (content management system), an internal messaging channel, internal newsletters, or even internal multimedia such as podcasts and video updates. What's important is that this information sharing becomes a habitual part of your organizational culture.

Sales' Role in Content Marketing

We'll explore the concept and importance of content marketing in detail later. However, it's essential to mention now because it's central to how Sales and Marketing should share information. So what exactly should Sales share with Marketing? The answer is anything that provides insight into the customer's perspective.

For example, if the Sales team notices that a specific product feature is consistently confusing customers, they should share that with Marketing. This allows Marketing to develop content that clarifies the feature or addresses the concern. A product issue may not always be an issue with the product itself—it could simply be how the company communicates usage and purpose of the product.

Similarly, if Sales hears repeated concerns from prospects about a particular industry challenge, that's valuable information for Marketing. It's an opportunity to create targeted content that addresses that challenge and positions your company as a thought leader.

Remember, this isn't a one-way street. While we're focusing on Sales-to-Marketing communication, the reverse is also essential. As we'll cover in a moment, Marketing should also provide feedback to Sales based on their analysis of campaign results, customer engagement, and market research.

However, the main point here is that you learn to utilize the rich, first-hand insight that Sales teams gain from their position to listen and have direct interactions with prospects. Incorporating this into your marketing strategies can significantly increase the effectiveness of your lead generation and nurturing, making your business more customer-centric and, ultimately, more successful.

To provide actionable steps and deeper understanding, let's break down the process of Sales-to-Marketing communication into specific actions.

1. Develop a System for Sharing Sales Insight

While ad hoc sharing of information can have its benefits, it's far more productive to establish a formalized system. This could be a shared digital dashboard where salespeople can log insights from their interactions with prospects, a regular meeting to discuss insights, or even a simple email chain. The important thing is that the system is easy to use, consistently utilized, and accessible to all relevant parties. If a company has already invested in a CRM, this is the best place to start. However, because CRM data is typically sectioned into individual customer information, using an open team collaboration system may be more efficient for the general cataloging of non-customer-specific insights and documents.

2. Highlight Customer Language and Objections

Salespeople should pay particular attention to the specific language prospects use when discussing their needs or problems. As well, any recurring objections to your product or service should be flagged for the Marketing team to address in their content. For example, when a customer says to a salesperson, "I need an easier way to pay my bill," Marketing can respond with messaging such as "Easy Bill Payment!" Another example would be if customers complain of a poor user interface in a software platform. This is a signal to Marketing to begin messaging about the new interface coming or to create a compelling defense explaining why your software is better than the company with the shiny new interface.

3. Provide Regular Feedback

This communication shouldn't be sporadic or reserved for "big" insights. Regular, ongoing feedback is central to catching trends and shifts in the market as they occur. With most communication being digital (websites, emails, social, texts), Marketing is able to pivot and change messages instantly. Your brand should be able to communicate back to the market in real time; however, to do this, you must have a clear and frequent understanding of changes in the market or industry. Sometimes these changes can be as subtle as the language your prospective customers are using to describe their viewpoint of your product.

To illustrate, let's consider an example. Think about a company that sells advanced construction hardware tools.

Example

As your Sales team is talking to prospects and customers, they start to notice a recurring theme. Many customers are expressing concerns about the safety of using power tools. They frequently use phrases like "avoiding accidents," "safety training," and "proper handling."

These insights are brought back to the Marketing team. Now they have the specifics: The customers' concerns are about safety in using power tools, and now we know the exact language they use when discussing your tools.

With these insights the Marketing team can create targeted content that addresses these specific concerns. This could include blog posts like, "The Essential Guide to Avoiding Accidents with Power Tools," or "Proper Handling of Power Tools: A Safety Primer."

Maybe the Marketing folks could create an infographic detailing safety measures when using the company's power tools or even a video tutorial called "Safety Training: How to Use [Your Company's Power Tool] Safely and Efficiently."

By creating content that uses the customers' own language to address their specific concerns, the company positions itself as attentive to customer needs and proactive in providing solutions. This establishes trust and directly addresses the factors that influence the purchasing decisions of prospects, increasing the effectiveness of the company's marketing efforts.

By addressing the specific pain point using the prospects' language, you're showing an understanding of their problem and offering a solution. This fosters trust and aligns your product as a solution to their specific needs, enhancing your lead-nurturing process and increasing the likelihood of conversion.

Example

Here's another example. Let's take a look at a company that owns and operates an event facility.

Your Sales team consistently hears from prospects that they're concerned about the "flow" of an event. They use terms like "smooth transitions," "proper layout," and "guest movement." They're particularly anxious about ensuring their guests move smoothly from one event segment to the next, such as from a cocktail hour to a seated dinner, or from a keynote speech to breakout sessions.

When the Sales team shares this concern and the specific language used by the prospects with the Marketing team, they're providing

Marketing with a powerful tool. Now the Marketing team knows the concerns are about the "flow" of events and the specific phrases clients are using involve "smooth transitions," "proper layout," and "guest movement."

With this insight, the Marketing team can create content that directly addresses these pain points and uses the clients' own language. They might create blog posts titled, "Ensuring Smooth Transitions at Your Event," or, "Designing Your Event for Optimal Guest Movement."

Perhaps the team could develop a downloadable guide or infographic titled, "The Art of Event Flow: How to Plan Your Layout for Smooth Transitions," or even produce a virtual tour video of the company's facility, demonstrating various layout options to optimize guest movement.

By addressing these concerns directly, the company assures potential clients that it understands and can handle their needs and also positions itself as an expert resource in successful event planning. This approach enhances lead generation, engagement, and, ultimately, conversions, as the company is speaking directly to the needs and language of its prospects.

Remember, the key to successful Sales-to-Marketing communication is consistency and actionability. Making that a regular part of your operations and ensuring that the insights shared translate into tangible changes in your marketing strategy are what will drive its success.

Show Me the Money—Leads versus Opportunities

It's not uncommon for Marketing to successfully bring in leads only to find out the leads that were targeted don't fit the types of leads likely to result in revenue generation. This is also a symptom of poor communication from Sales to Marketing.

When marketers are pressured to deliver more leads yet are not a part of the sales conversation, we easily become obsessed with the lead quantity goal. This, of course, results in focusing on amassing as many leads as possible, believing that a higher quantity will naturally translate to a higher number of conversions.

However, this belief can sometimes lead us astray, taking us on a wild goose chase where we're attracting leads that don't align with our most profitable customer profile or our best product-customer fit. The reality is, more leads do not always equate to the right customers or the most profitable outcomes.

For the Marketing team, one main piece of this puzzle that can be overlooked is how they understand which customers and which products are the most profitable. They need this information to fine-tune their strategies and direct their efforts toward attracting the right leads. But where does this understanding come from? This is where it's the Sales team's responsibility to step in and clearly communicate this customer understanding to Marketing.

This is not Sales doing a Marketing job. This is not a place for the Sales team's ego either. It is the place where Sales transfers knowledge to another part of the revenue generation machine.

Our Sales teams hold valuable insights from their direct interaction with the customers. They have their finger on the pulse of the market, understanding who our profitable customers are, which products they prefer, and why they find those products valuable. They understand the nuances of product-customer fit, knowing firsthand what solutions our customers need and which of our products meet those needs the best. This information is priceless, but only if it's shared and put into action.

To make the most of these insights, the Sales team needs to actively communicate their experiences and data gathered from customer interactions to the Marketing team. For instance, if the Sales team recognizes that customers from the manufacturing industry find a product line to be particularly valuable due to its durability and efficiency, then these two data points need to be passed on to the Marketing team. The marketers can then create targeted campaigns that highlight the durability and efficiency of the product, specifically addressing manufacturing industry professionals who are concerned with durability and efficiency.

Similarly, if the Sales team identifies that customers within a specific demographic or region tend to yield higher profits, the Marketing team needs this information. Marketing can then tailor their strategies to attract more leads fitting those two customer data points—demographic and region.

As you can see, this collaboration between Sales and Marketing has a goal better than acquiring more leads; it has the more effective goal of acquiring the right leads. It ensures that our marketing efforts are congruent with the type of prospect that is likely to convert into a customer—and not just any customer, but a profitable one. It ensures that we're using our resources effectively and targeting those prospects that offer us the greatest return on our investment.

Simply put, it's about having more profitable leads. And to accomplish this, it's essential that the Sales team communicates effectively with the Marketing team, sharing insights about profitable customers and product-customer fits. Remember, the goal is not to create leads, nor is it just to increase conversions. The goal is to maximize profitability—and that begins with targeting the right leads.

The Cold Call Is Coming from Inside the House

There's more to Sales-to-Marketing communication than talking about new and unknown prospects. Since our focus is on profitability and not on leads, we now have to address the fact that sometimes our most profitable opportunities come from existing customers. With tactics such as "land and expand" and account-based marketing (ABM) in play, it is possible that the most profitable customers are already in hand. "Land and expand" refers to getting in the door with a small deal and then working your way into the company to sell larger deals. This is similar to account-based marketing, except that ABM could happen leading up to or after an opportunity exists. Communication is key here because often Sales may know that the profits come from existing customers, while Marketing is overfocused on converting unknown leads to known ones. In this case, efforts are better spent on nurturing, educating, and informing existing customers. It costs a lot less to convince existing customers to buy more than it does to find new customers and convince them to buy.

I've had firsthand experiences of being frustrated about why Sales wasn't concerned with helping to bring in new leads. The reality was that they were more likely to be compensated for bringing new business from existing customers. Marketing could have helped had this understanding been clear.

This communication requirement also extends to products. What happens when Marketing is focused on new products while Sales knows that the old version is helping more to meet quota? The result is that their efforts become misaligned along with their goals. We will get deeper into the alignment issues as well as the impact of separate goals later. The point here is that communication can avoid this crack in Sales and Marketing cohesion, or at least prevent it from getting worse.

Communication That Closes the Deal

In business, every successfully closed deal is a well of untapped knowledge. However, the valuable insights gained from these successful negotiations often remain confined to the Sales department. This is a missed opportunity. The insights from Sales' victories hold the potential to equip the Marketing team with precise knowledge that can help refine their strategies and propel the business forward.

Consider this scenario: The Sales team has just closed a deal with a major client after a series of meetings and negotiations. The salesperson, Jack, is aware of the nuances that drove the deal to fruition. Jack knows that the client was drawn to a particular feature of the company's construction software that its competitor lacked—a feature that allows users to simulate different environmental impacts on their construction plans.

Now imagine if Jack shares this insight with the Marketing team. The team can then highlight this feature prominently in their promotional content, thereby attracting other potential clients who may be seeking the same capability. There is a direct connection that must be formed between sales knowledge and marketing strategy, yet it's often overlooked.

For this to work effectively, we need to establish a protocol of communication. Every time a deal closes, the salesperson should brief the Marketing team about the specifics of the deal. The details of the product or service sold, the unique selling points that attracted the client, any objections that were raised and addressed, and the factors that finally led the client to sign—all these pieces of information can be invaluable for the Marketing team.

Beyond transmitting information, we must now translate this information into actionable strategies. The Marketing team should scrutinize these details, identify patterns, and use the insights to refine their marketing strategy. Whether it's adjusting the buyer persona, refining the message, tweaking the ad targeting, or enhancing the product presentation on the company's website, every piece of information can help make their marketing efforts more accurate and effective.

Remember, the goal here is to foster a strong Sales-to-Marketing feedback loop. When Sales understands how Marketing warms up leads to prepare for negotiation and Marketing uses Sales' insights to improve their strategies, business performance improves significantly.

Here are some actionable insights that a Sales team can communicate to a Marketing team regarding a closed deal:

Details of the Prospect: Share basic information such as the industry, company size, role of the key decision-maker, and geographical location. This helps Marketing fine-tune their buyer persona and better target their campaigns.

Buying Triggers: What was the specific problem or need that led the prospect to seek a solution? Understanding these buying triggers can help Marketing craft more relevant messages.

Sales Process: How many interactions or touchpoints did it take to close the deal? This can provide insights into the prospect's buying journey, helping Marketing align their content to different stages of this journey.

Unique Selling Points: Which features or benefits of the product or service were most appealing to the prospect? This information can help Marketing highlight these selling points in their promotional efforts.

Competitive Advantage: Was there something that set your product or service apart from the competition in the eyes of the prospect? Understanding this can help Marketing strengthen your company's unique value proposition.

Objections Overcome: What were the main concerns or objections raised by the prospect and how were they addressed? This information can help Marketing create content that preemptively addresses these objections.

Follow-Up Questions: What questions did the prospect ask after the deal was closed? These could reveal potential areas for improvement in the way the product or service is presented.

By sharing this information, the Sales team can equip the Marketing team with real-world insights that can help Marketing optimize their strategies and generate more quality leads. Remember, every deal closed is an opportunity for learning and improvement. When Sales and Marketing work together in this manner, they can create a powerful synergy that drives growth and profitability.

Communicating Respect for Marketing's Role

We cannot discuss communication among Marketing and Sales team members without talking about communication on a personal level. Beyond team operations, we are talking about the individual communication and requests between people on these teams.

At the root of the relationship between the Marketing and Sales teams is how they perceive the value of each other's team. Because Sales is nearly synonymous with profit, Marketing can be seen as playing more of a supporting role. Now that the customer journey is nearly completely in the customer's hands, Marketing must be seen as an equal partner in the revenue generation process.

Mutual respect is a cornerstone of effective collaboration between Sales and Marketing. Before we go deeper, let's first examine some tasks that Sales teams often delegate to Marketing that might be considered menial:

1. Creating or updating sales presentations

2. Making minor updates to the company website

3. Generating one-off reports that have little strategic value

4. Designing event invitations or other promotional materials

5. Drafting routine customer correspondence

6. Conducting basic customer research that is readily available

The list can go on and on. The point is that Sales must value Marketing as a part of the revenue generation team—not the creative or "make it pretty" team.

Organizations that fail to understand the value of Marketing within the revenue process can easily fall into the "Sales Is King" entitlement trap. This scenario is so common that it was satirized in the NBC television show The Office, where an episode was appropriately titled "New Leads." The result of this trap is that we don't look to other parts of the organization until the pipeline begins to dry up. Then, suddenly, Marketing becomes the focus of finding those new leads.

We can recognize that the Sales department closes deals and finalizes the accounting of revenue. However, it's important to also recognize that Marketing is equally as vital to the revenue-generating operations of a business. It's a critical cog in the revenue wheel, working relentlessly to continuously fuel the sales pipeline with quality leads, enhancing brand perception, and ensuring that customers are engaged and satisfied.

A company's Marketing department is its strategic powerhouse. Marketing teams use their industry insights, creativity, and strategic thinking to craft campaigns that resonate with customers. They engage audiences, shape brand narratives, and drive awareness to ultimately generate demand. They analyze market trends, competitor strategies, and customer behavior, and use these insights to position the company favorably in a competitive landscape. They're not just the "arts and crafts" department— they're pivotal to driving the business forward.

When Sales views Marketing as simply a supporting function or dismisses their work as "menial," it creates a divide. This can result in reduced collaboration, poor alignment, and a lack of shared goals—all of which can ultimately impact a company's bottom line.

To foster a better relationship and to demonstrate trust and respect toward the Marketing team, here are some actions that Sales can take:

Understand Marketing's Role: Attend Marketing's meetings and take part in their initiatives to gain a better understanding of the work Marketing does and the value they bring.

Communicate Clearly: Be clear about what you need from Marketing. Don't hastily dump tasks on them; explain the strategic importance of what you're asking for.

Acknowledge the Work Marketing Does: Give credit where credit is due. If a marketing campaign resulted in successful leads, acknowledge it.

Provide Constructive Feedback: If there's something you're not satisfied with, provide constructive feedback. Make it a discussion on how to improve rather than just criticism.

Show Interest in Marketing's Success Metrics: Just like sales quotas, Marketing has KPIs they're trying to meet. Show interest in these and understand how they relate to Sales' goals.

Involve Marketing in Strategic Conversations: If there's a shift in the sales strategy or a new target market, involve Marketing in these discussions. Their input can be valuable.

Valuing and respecting the role of Marketing within a business is a must for any company that wants to increase its revenue. After all, a chain is only as strong as its weakest link. By recognizing the strategic importance of Marketing, Sales can help forge a stronger link that drives the company forward.

Expert Insight—Mark Schaefer

Mark Schaefer is a globally recognized keynote speaker, educator, business consultant, and author with over 30 years of experience in global sales, PR, and marketing. He has held significant roles in corporate sales and marketing, working with clients ranging from start-ups to global brands. Mark is also a prolific author of 10 best-selling books and a faculty member at Rutgers University, where he shares his extensive knowledge of marketing and organizational development.

Mark shares a specific story that provides insight into how Sales and Marketing can go beyond the boardroom to share customer activities that foster alignment and strengthen connections between the teams:

I was in sales for eight years. And I was highly trusted because I had a senior sales position. I knew the ins and outs of the customers, the products, the challenges, the frustrations that our Sales team faced. And so as I moved into a senior marketing position, I was completely trusted because I was seen like I was one of them. They were my friends. They trusted me, but I also trusted them because I knew they were good people trying to do a good job. And that really helped the relationship. So I can say that in my role as a senior marketing manager, I literally had no problems with misalignment with our Sales team because of that trust I had earned over many, many years.

There is one thing we did that I think was unique. Every other year, we conducted a formal listen-to-the-customer activity. This was a very in-depth, serious process where it would always be a team of three people. There would be me, there would be an account manager, and there would be someone from our technical group. And we actually went through training so that we could listen well. And the reason we always had three people on these visits is because we wanted three different perspectives. We wanted Sales, we wanted Marketing, and we wanted technology, because we wanted to hear and understand if there were any technical problems, if there were any quality problems, if there were any product development opportunities.

We actually went through a training program to learn how to conduct these sessions. The session would probably last about an hour each customer. The reason we only did this every other year is because it was a major investment of time and money—because we would literally go and visit our major customers all around the world. It was quite an investment, and we felt like every other year was probably good enough.

And what we found in these listening visits: First of all, our customers really appreciated this. They loved the fact that we would go to this effort, this very valuable effort, to get in tune with what their needs were, where they thought the industry was going, what they aspired to grow into in the future. And so we kind of had a halo effect from just doing the activity.

The second valuable thing that came out of this is that we had a competitive advantage because we heard things in those meetings that put us on a path to be months or sometimes years ahead of our competitors, because we were out there listening to the customers with this intent.

The third thing that happened was that it created a very strong alignment between Sales and Marketing because we were partners in this project. They were right in the meeting with us. They were hearing the same things we were hearing from the customers. They were accountable afterward to manage some of the projects that came out of this so there was really no misunderstanding. Because, after the listening session, the three of us would get together and write our notes. So it was clear; it was unified. And for every single customer, we had a vision of what we needed to do from a Sales side, from a Marketing side, and from a technical side that helped us serve that customer. And so again, that was another thing that I think really contributed to this idea of Sales and Marketing alignment. I can't remember a single incident where we had any misalignment because we were so connected through our relationships and also through these listening visits.

Chapter 3

Marketing-to-Sales Communication

In the last chapter, we discussed the intricacies of Sales communicating to Marketing, highlighting the importance of a shared language and collaboration. Now we're shifting our attention to a different yet equally essential direction of the conversation: Marketing-to-Sales communication.

While it might seem like a subtle difference, it's an essential one. This chapter will guide you through various topics, from understanding the digital footprints of prospects to appreciating the power of marketing data. We'll explore how Marketing keeps Sales in the loop and how Sales can better grasp the hidden value in the often-overlooked "administrative" tasks.

Each section will unfold insights and practices that can enhance the collaboration between Marketing and Sales, paving the way for a more cohesive and profitable organization. It's time we take a closer look at the relationship from the other side of the mirror.

Informing Sales of Digital Activity

Marketing's role in understanding the customer journey is complex and vital. Armed with tools and techniques that meticulously trace the digital activities of prospects, Marketing teams build an intricate map of where customers have been and where they might be going. However, here's where a common disconnect emerges: This invaluable digital footprint data often remains confined within the marketing systems, even after new leads are handed over to Sales for further qualification.

Why does this occur, and what can be done to bridge this divide? We will discuss the systems in a later chapter, but for now, let's address how to communicate through and eliminate the silo. Marketing is more likely to be concerned with examining the data that lays out the entire customer journey. Sales, on the other hand, is typically more concerned with immediate bottom-line activity, such as closing a new deal.

I was forced to clearly explain the difference between Sales and Marketing activity when a very special person challenged me with this question:

> My mother is in her eighties, and although she is highly educated and still very sharp intellectually, she doesn't totally understand what I do for a living.
>
> She asked me a very interesting question. She said, "What is the difference between a marketer and a salesperson?"
>
> To put it in a context that she would quickly pick up on, I answered:
>
> A marketer looks at you and says, "She has bought a new car every five years, it's always a Cadillac, and she gets her car serviced regularly at the Cadillac dealership. Let's make sure she keeps buying a Cadillac and comes to us when it's time."
>
> A salesperson says, "So. Has it been five years? If not, don't bother me."
>
> My mother chuckled and said, "Ha, I get it!"

Now she has a better idea of what I do.

Sales teams, driven by the immediate needs and demands of closing deals, may not always recognize the value of the digital information that Marketing teams have painstakingly gathered. The intricate details of how prospects navigated a website, the ads they clicked on, or the content they engaged with might seem peripheral. However, these seemingly minor details can reveal deep insights into a prospect's needs, pain points, and interests.

Here is where transparent communication and collaboration flowing from Marketing to Sales comes in—starting with these steps:

Share the Tools: Marketing can grant Sales access to the platforms where the data resides or create regular reports that highlight key digital activities of leads and prospects.

Educate Each Other: Marketing should take the lead in educating Sales about how to interpret the data and why it's essential to understanding customer intent and behavior.

Incorporate What Was Learned into Sales Processes: Sales should be encouraged to integrate this information into their selling strategies, tailoring their approach based on the insights gleaned from a prospect's digital footprint.

Schedule Regular Check-Ins: Scheduled meetings between Marketing and Sales to discuss trends and particular cases can keep the information flow fresh and relevant.

Why should Sales care? Because Marketing often knows more about the potential next customer than Sales does.

As a salesperson, you certainly don't want to walk into a sales meeting or open a sales call without having in hand all available data regarding the customer journey. Or worse, imagine if the customer just finished viewing a white paper, attending a webinar, or downloading a product guide and you, the salesperson, open a call with the customer as if they had just now heard of your company. That call would not go well.

Understanding the digital activities of prospects is a powerful means of aligning sales strategies with actual customer behavior. It informs Sales of what resonates with prospects and what doesn't. This knowledge in turn empowers Sales to engage prospects with more targeted and relevant messages, thereby enhancing the likelihood of a successful conversion.

Turning the Customer Journey into Conversions

Understanding the intricacies of the customer journey is no longer confined to the Marketing department. As we move through the digital customer journey, Sales must tap into the known customer sentiment, experience, and activity trends. This is where we go beyond numbers and start looking at the psychology of the customers during their journey.

Customers express themselves digitally through their choices, their interactions, their likes and dislikes—all signaled by views, listens, and clicks. Marketing has the tools to unravel these digital expressions, but if all these insights remain locked away in a marketing platform, we are shortchanging our Sales team. We are restricting their ability to connect, engage, and resonate with the prospects in the most effective way.

Consider it this way: The Marketing team paints a vivid picture of what the customer feels, wants, and expects. Now, what if the Sales team had access to this gallery of insights? Wouldn't it empower them to approach customers with a tailored, empathetic strategy that's aligned with their needs and emotions?

As we break down the communication silos and open the communication channels, we encourage Sales to step into the world that Marketing has already discovered. Sharing this information should not be viewed as a tedious task. It is a strategic move and, more importantly, a means to align our efforts for common wins.

Regarding marketing content, too often this content is tucked away in storage, somewhere in a CMS (content management system), on the website, in the marketing automation platform, or even in the email marketing system.

Here's where we must foster a two-way street of communication and collaboration. Marketing can shine a spotlight on this content, creating an accessible archive and routinely updating Sales about new additions as well as reminding them of evergreen content. Marketing can arrange briefings, share newsletters, or employ internal platforms to ensure that these resources are not just available but announced and visible.

And Sales? They must intentionally seek this information and hold Marketing accountable for sharing it. Sales should make a regular habit of researching content archives, asking questions, engaging with the Marketing team, and understanding how to leverage this content for their jobs. Sales may not attempt to be informed, although they should be actively seeking, absorbing, and applying this knowledge. It is Marketing's responsibility to drive this communication, and as a result Sales can enrich their conversations with customers and align themselves with the vision and voice of Marketing.

I can't stress enough that it takes effort from both teams. For Marketing to successfully share this information, Sales must crave these insights, recognize their value, and integrate them into their strategies. Marketing must act as the guide and the mentor, delivering these insights with clarity and purpose. Together, they can turn customer sentiment and activity trends into a winning playbook, an approach that's both data-driven and psychology-driven. A human approach to a digital world. That's where we find the true connection. That's where we begin to convert prospects into customers.

The Administrative Devil—Communicating Data

I once had a salesperson tell me that he was not going to stop what he was doing to "put all that data into Salesforce, that's administrative work!" By the end of the quarter, similar salespeople were complaining that Marketing brought them leads that were not converting. There is a clear connection here—let me explain.

Imagine you're a navigator steering a ship through uncharted waters. The more information you have about the currents, weather patterns, and obstacles, the smoother and more precise your journey. In Sales and Marketing, the data entered by salespeople into a CRM like Salesforce is akin to this vital navigational information. Unfortunately, this is where we encounter another disconnect.

Often salespeople view the task of entering data into the CRM as low-value "administrative" work, almost like an anchor slowing them down. But let's dissect this notion, because within it lies a profound insight.

This data is a road map to a prospect's mind. It informs Marketing about the prospect's needs, interests, and pain points. This granularity empowers Marketing to create targeted and relevant content that resonates with prospects, pushing them smoothly through the sales process.

Now let's navigate this together. Sales offers insights and reports on customer interactions. Meanwhile, Marketing lays down the content to guide the customer. Together, they navigate as well as guide the prospect's journey. Suppose the salesperson doesn't communicate interactions by entering the data into the CRM? The less data they have, the more difficult the journey. A missed detail here, a generalized assumption there, and the opportunity to close the deal falters. The impact on the prospect diminishes, and the opportunity may be lost.

So how do we forge this symbiotic relationship between Sales and Marketing? It starts with a shift in perspective. The members of the Sales team must view entering data into the CRM as a strategic action toward helping them close the deal. It's about laying down the breadcrumbs for Marketing to follow, craft, and complement the Sales efforts.

Certainly the balance between traditional sales activities and data entry might seem like a tightrope walk for salespeople. How do we bridge this gap without losing sight of the core responsibilities?

Here's a way salespeople can accomplish these essential tasks:

> **Schedule Time Blocks:** Allocate specific blocks of time in your daily or weekly routine solely for data entry. By creating a designated window you ensure this task doesn't become an overwhelming chore but rather an integral part of your workflow.
>
> **Leverage Technology:** Utilize tools and software that integrate with your CRM, which can automate specific data entry tasks. For instance, connecting your email system might auto-populate

essential information, cutting down on manual work. Or use the mobile app version of your CRM to enter information as it happens.

Balance Quality and Quantity: Focus on entering the most critical information that will directly impact Marketing's ability to nurture leads. Instead of getting bogged down by every detail, highlight the core insights that really matter. This does not mean only entering what matters to you! It means entering what matters to the overall sales process, including data that will assist Marketing's targeting efforts.

Educate and Collaborate with Marketing: Communicate with your Marketing team to understand exactly what information they need. The more aligned you are, the more precise your data entry can become, eliminating unnecessary work.

Create a Supportive Culture: Encourage a workplace culture where data entry is recognized and rewarded. Leadership can play a significant role in emphasizing the importance of this task and celebrating those who excel in it.

Monitor and Assess: Regularly assess how much time you're spending on data entry and adjust accordingly. If it's becoming a burden, consider internal resources, artificial intelligence tools, automation, or third-party services that might assist with this task.

By integrating these practices, salespeople can find a rhythm that maintains the essence of their traditional roles and nurtures a seamless collaboration with Marketing. This isn't a divergence from the path; it's an enhancement, a richer layer that connects the efforts of Sales and Marketing and ultimately leads to more successful engagements with prospects.

Chapter 4

Closing the Communication Loop

Marketing creates content. Content attracts leads. Leads are pursued by salespeople who field any objections. Objections are used by Marketing to enhance lead-nurturing campaigns. Lead-nurturing campaigns move leads into opportunities. Opportunities worked by both Sales and Marketing lead to deals. Deals are examined to create similar deals and generate more business from the same customers. This is what happens when the communication loop is strategically closed and working effectively.

This communication loop summarizes all that we have discussed in the *Communication* portion of the CASH framework.

The described communication loop between Marketing and Sales is a systematic, interconnected process that ensures the seamless flow of leads through the sales funnel. It also supports bringing those leads that leak through the side of the funnel back into the funnel. Let's break down how this loop operates and what actions can be taken to ensure that it is functioning effectively:

> **Content Creation by Marketing:** Marketing's role begins with crafting valuable content that resonates with potential customers. This content acts as a magnet, drawing prospects in. The key here

is creating content that speaks directly to the needs and interests of the target audience.

Lead Attraction and Pursuit by Sales: Once leads are attracted, Sales takes over, engaging with these prospects, understanding their needs, and fielding any objections. Sales must be informed about the content created by Marketing, using it as an educational tool to overcome objections.

Marketing-Enhancing, Lead-Nurturing Campaigns: The objections and insights gathered by Sales are communicated back to Marketing. This information is crucial, as Marketing can refine their lead-nurturing campaigns to address common concerns or misconceptions.

Transformation into Opportunities: With more targeted and refined nurturing, leads are converted into opportunities. Sales and Marketing work in unison here, utilizing shared insights, content, and strategies to persuade and convert.

Here are actions that your teams can take to ensure that the communication loop is fully closed and effective:

Regular Communication Channels: Set up regular meetings between Sales and Marketing to discuss ongoing campaigns, lead behavior, and objections faced. This will help in adjusting strategies in real time.

Shared Tools and Platforms: Use shared platforms like a CRM where both Sales and Marketing can access and update information about leads and customers. This ensures that data is accessible to all relevant parties and not siloed into team-specific platforms.

Defined Processes and Responsibilities: Clearly outline who is responsible for what at each stage of the loop and what the communication expectations are. Whether it's about informing Sales about the latest content or Sales providing feedback on lead objections, everyone must know their role.

Performance Metrics and Review: Regularly review the effectiveness of the communication loop through specific metrics like lead conversion rate, sales cycle length, or customer satisfaction. Adjust strategies as needed based on these insights.

Let's consider a prime example of the communication loop at work, one that I personally witnessed unfold.

Example

A software company was on the verge of launching an innovative artificial intelligence (AI) tool. It was a time filled with anticipation, with both Sales and Marketing teams gearing up for the challenge. They knew their collaboration would be key.

As a marketing leader, I found myself in close partnership with Oren, the head of Sales. My team and I had been busily preparing content and research to attract potential customers. Oren's team, on the other hand, was set to engage with the leads we would generate.

The product hit the market and Marketing's targeted campaigns began to attract many interested leads. Oren was attentive, gathering insights about the prospects' needs and objections from his team's calls. In regular meetings with the Marketing team and me, he would share this crucial information.

We absorbed his insights and adjusted our nurture campaigns to become more refined and targeted. Our continuous collaboration with Sales allowed us to improve our nurturing effectiveness, tailoring the content to speak directly to each prospect's specific needs.

This exchange of information continued to thrive, with a seamless flow of understanding between Sales and Marketing. Sales' insights into the prospects' needs and objections guided Marketing's adjustments in content and messaging.

The outcome was synergy: Marketing, now armed with firsthand knowledge, could support Sales with incredibly tailored content. Sales, in turn, could close deals more effectively.

And when those deals were sealed, they stood as proof of what can be achieved through a tightly knit, strategically coordinated communication loop between Sales and Marketing. It was a victory for the power of true collaboration.

Closing the communication loop between Sales and Marketing is essential for the efficiency and success of both teams. It leads to more cohesive strategies, a better understanding of the customer, and, ultimately, more successful and profitable deals.

The actions above contribute to and sustain this closed loop, fostering an environment where Sales and Marketing are not separate entities but collaborative partners in a shared mission.

Part 2

C

<u>A</u>lignment

S

H

One might say this whole book is about alignment. However, alignment is just one part of bringing Sales and Marketing together to perform as one. Two railroad tracks can be perfectly aligned for thousands of miles, but that alone does not accomplish getting a train to its goal. There is communication in the form of traffic coordination. There are systems that manage the mechanics and movements. And there are people who have the responsibility of managing it all. When the rails go out of alignment, it indicates failures of those other parts—and the train crashes. When in alignment, this part of the process is effective; however, the train doesn't move without the communication of the other moving parts and the mechanical systems to move it.

Alignment is crucial, but again, is only one of the four essential keys in bringing Sales and Marketing together as a revenue-generating machine.

Alignment between Sales and Marketing is necessary to create a unified and effective Revenue team. The next few chapters explore how understanding roles, sharing key performance indicators (KPIs), and building a supportive organizational culture drive this alignment. Recognizing and respecting each team's contributions helps break down silos and work toward common objectives.

Part 2 provides practical strategies and insights to help Sales and Marketing teams operate as a cohesive unit. Embracing alignment leads to better communication, improved efficiency, and greater success in achieving shared goals.

Chapter 5

Understanding Sales and Marketing Roles

As Chris and I shifted through the desks and closets used by the previous Marketing team, we came across a box of plastic pork chops. For the life of us, we could not figure out what kind of marketing campaign could have called for a software company to need plastic pork chops. I'm sure there was some creative idea to combine this chew toy with selling software. However, to this day it represents in my mind how the Sales team viewed the Marketing team. Marketing was the team that wasted money on gimmicks and things to give away at trade shows. Things like plastic pork chops.

Fortunately, in many organizations the relationship between Sales and Marketing has transformed both drastically and quietly in the digital age. But not all have grasped the seismic shift that's taken place.

Business has grown past the days when Marketing's role could be accurately perceived as the architects of websites, orchestrators of events, creators of logos, and designers of T-shirts. The age-old demand from Sales to Marketing was simple: "Generate leads, and we'll handle the rest." However, that notion fails to recognize the complex and critical role Marketing plays today.

With the advent of the internet and the resulting digital revolution, the customer journey fundamentally changed. Sales no longer controls and guides the customer through a prescribed path. The customer has basically told businesses, "I am the captain now." Customers now set their own courses, armed with endless information and choices, often initiating their journeys online. And who guides them through this labyrinth? It's Marketing, not Sales, that holds the map.

> *Side Note:* Some organizations hold Marketing content back by demanding each piece of knowledge be gated so they can collect leads. However, the harsh truth is that your customers will learn what they need from somewhere—whether from you or your competitor—without giving up an email address or completing a form to get it.

In an era where the customers control their journey toward purchasing, we have to remember that Marketing's role goes far beyond lead generation. It's about nurturing, educating, and influencing potential customers through carefully crafted content, targeted campaigns, and insightful research that is readily and easily accessible to the customer. It's an orchestration of various strategies that align with the prospect's needs, objections, and aspirations. Marketing's ability to influence the customer journey has never been more profound or more misunderstood.

Sales, focused on the ultimate goal of closing deals, can sometimes overlook Marketing's multifaceted value. It's essential for Sales to recognize that the customer journey is no longer a straight line, but a complex web. Marketing's role extends throughout the entire buying process and is not confined to the top of the funnel.

In many ways, Marketing has become the unseen hand that guides prospects through the initial stages of awareness and consideration, right up to the very brink of decision-making. Cohesion between Sales and Marketing is crucial to understanding and speaking the customers' language, preempting their concerns, and responding to their needs. It's about being present where the customers are (often online), providing the information, assurance, and encouragement they seek. We must then consistently nurture those leads with the right content at the right time through the right channels until the deal is done.

Although the movement of prospect responsibility is no longer a direct or final handoff between Marketing and Sales, Marketing's role is to ensure that when a lead is handed over to Sales, it is a well-profiled and truly interested prospect.

So, does Sales understand the value of Marketing? If not, it's time for a mindset shift. A fresh understanding of what Marketing truly represents in a modern customer-led buying landscape. It's about recognizing Marketing as an integral, strategic partner in the entire sales process. It's time to look beyond the websites, events, logos, and T-shirts (and plastic pork chops) and see the real power and potential that lies within the hands of Marketing. The future of your company revenue depends on the understanding and leveraging of this partnership.

The Role of Marketing: Dispelling the Sales Perception

The evolution of marketing has been profound, going beyond traditional concepts such as brand building, advertising, lead generation, and demand generation. Modern marketing encompasses an array of strategies, technologies, and channels that might not align with what Sales traditionally perceives as Marketing's function. This misalignment can hinder communication and collaboration between the two departments. To help dispel these misconceptions, let's review a few facets of modern Marketing.

Understanding Your Audience

One of the most crucial elements of Marketing is clearly and specifically knowing who your audience should be. Defining and selecting the right audience can make the difference between a successful campaign and a missed opportunity. The next step is understanding that audience enough to attract them. Marketers like to use the term "targeting" to define the activity of pinpointing the exact people they want to connect to. Another perspective is "farming." This means that you plant value in the path of prospective customers, cultivate relationships, and then harvest the business as a result.

Expert Insight—Seth Godin

Seth Godin is a renowned author, entrepreneur, and marketing expert known for his influential ideas on leadership, innovation, and the digital age. Seth and I discussed the definition of modern Marketing as well as ideal ways to understand and reach an audience. In Seth's words:

Most people think Marketing is hype and hustle and advertising and promotion and getting the word out. It's a selfish activity based on the belief that if you could just interrupt enough people, you could make enough money to interrupt enough people. And that works, if you're one of the only people who are doing it.

But in the last 20 years, with the explosion of free media, with the ability of every individual to show up in front of other people, clearly, scarce attention has been strip-mined to the point where Marketing in the old way doesn't make any sense. So I think modern Marketing is the privilege, the chance, to help people get to where they want to go. Not to steal their attention, but to earn their enrollment and the benefit of the doubt.

And if we have people's enrollment, it means they want to go somewhere, and they're likely to trust us—and then our job, pretty clearly, is to teach them; it is to say, "If you knew what I know, you would want to do this." And so what it means to become a marketer is to have a story, a true story, a story that holds up the scrutiny, that other people want to hear. And that only makes sense if you are only serving a few people. It's impossible to be a mass brand anymore. Salsa outsells ketchup, but it outsells ketchup because there's lots and lots and lots of kinds of salsa and only one kind of ketchup. You're not going to be able to make something that everybody wants.

I would say that "targeting" is a hunting term, and you're not a hunter. You're a farmer. And farmers have the choice of which field. They plant things, they fertilize them, they water them, and then they patiently wait for them to grow. And farmers don't use words like "target." The opportunity that you have is to say, "Where is there a fertile territory where I can add actual value?"

And I think demographics are an old-fashioned method that is only used by people who don't understand psychographics. Demographics are, "What do you look like and what's on your census form?" Psychographics are, "What do you believe? What do you want? What do you dream of?" And if I know you drive a pickup truck, that is way more interesting to me than knowing that you are a 45-year-old woman. And we need to find the choices that people are already choosing to make and then help their dreams come true.

To hear or view the rest of that engaging conversation with Seth, look up my podcast called *The Business of Marketing* with A. Lee Judge on YouTube or your preferred podcast platform.

Content Marketing

When I first began trying to explain content marketing to a Sales team member, I was hit with harsh pushback that was also a harsh reality. It was the first quarter (Q1) of the year. I explained that content marketing was the long game; the content we create today will drive pipeline growth and deals for Q4. His reply? "I'm measured by quarterly reports. If what I do today doesn't show results soon, I'll be fired by Q4!" He had a point that can't be ignored—so keep this frequent misalignment of measurement time frames in mind.

To help explain content marketing to a Sales team, it is important to stress that content marketing is more than producing attractive blog posts or engaging social media updates; it involves creating a bridge between the potential customer and the Sales team. For a salesperson, understanding and leveraging content marketing is like having an ally on the battlefield, assisting in identifying, engaging, and nurturing leads.

In 2017, while serving as a marketing executive, I began creating content for the software company I was working for. After seeing positive impact on the sales cycle, I was convinced that content had a direct effect on business in a way befitting the changing customer journey. The content was so compelling that I began getting requests from other companies to create types of content similar to what I created for my employer. I soon realized that the demand for business content was growing. As a result, I founded the content marketing company Content Monsta. You can learn more about that company at ContentMonsta.com (just don't forget that Monsta is spelled with an "a" at the end).

One of the strongest ways to express a company's ability to solve a customer problem is through content—rather than a sales pitch.

Imagine a prospect who's just realized she has a problem that needs solving. She goes online and searches for solutions, and among the results finds a well-crafted article from your company. This article does more than sell a product; it educates, enlightens, and aligns with the prospect's pain points. In essence, this piece of content has started the conversation that Sales will later continue.

The power of content marketing is in its ability to engage prospects at various stages of the buying cycle. For the Sales team, this means the initial barrier has already been broken. The trust building has begun, all thanks to a valuable piece of content that resonates with the prospect.

Content marketing enables Sales to step into a conversation that's already warmed up. Leads that come through content are often more informed, more engaged, and more open to what Sales has to say. That's because the content has already established a relationship, credibility, and a level of trust.

Here's where the synergy between Sales and Marketing truly shines. Sales can provide the people in Marketing with insights into the common questions, challenges, and objections they encounter. Marketing can then create content that addresses these aspects, effectively softening the ground for Sales. To achieve this, a strategic approach to content creation is essential.

A challenge that Marketing teams often face is the question of whether to focus on quality of content or quantity of content. It is a mistake to ask for or spend too much of a budget on the wrong part of the sales cycle. Yet attempting to create the quantity of content required to compete with competitor attention share can be costly without a strategy. Without a strategy, a Marketing team will be left with failed campaigns and a depleted budget with little action in the sales funnel to show for it.

For this reason, I've developed what I call the *"QvQ Content Funnel."* The QvQ Content Funnel, shown in Figure 5.1, matches marketing content to the traditional stages of the sales funnel while balancing quality and quantity of content at different stages of the funnel. This approach ensures your marketing content nurtures leads from awareness to action, optimizing engagement, conversion rates, and, most of all—budget. The goal is to achieve the QvQ *balance*—the balance between quantity and quality of content at the appropriate time within the customer journey.

The QvQ Content Funnel

Quality vs. Quantity

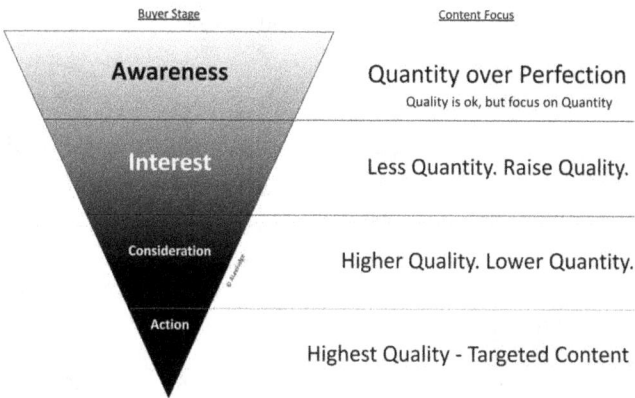

Figure 5.1 The QvQ Content Funnel

Now let's break down the types of content you should produce at each level, keeping in mind the balance of quantity versus quality.

Stage 1: Awareness

At the Awareness stage, the goal is to reach a broad audience and introduce that audience to your brand. Here quantity takes precedence over quality; however, that doesn't mean compromising on the latter. The key is to produce a high volume of engaging, easily consumable content that grabs attention quickly.

- **Content Types:** Short-form videos, blog articles, social media posts, infographics.

- **Strategy:** Use snippets from longer content (like podcasts or interviews) to create multiple short pieces. Focus on easily consumable and concise messaging. Capture conversational content for non-scripted and authentic communication.

- **Example:** A 30-second clip from a podcast featuring a key insight from an industry expert or customer shared across social media platforms to drive brand awareness.
- **Focus—Quantity over Perfection:** Quality is important, but the emphasis is on producing a large volume of content.

Stage 2: Interest

In the Interest stage, the focus shifts slightly toward quality while still maintaining a reasonable quantity of content. At this point, your audience has shown some interest and is willing to engage more deeply.

- **Content Types:** Longer videos, podcasts, newsletters, and webinars.
- **Strategy:** Produce content that offers more in-depth information. Use storytelling and detailed explanations to keep the audience engaged. Continue creating short-form content to drive interest.
- **Example:** A 10-minute YouTube video that expands on the short-form content, providing deeper insights and engaging storytelling.
- **Focus—Story and Emotional Connection:** Create content that builds a connection with your audience.

Stage 3: Consideration

As prospects move to the Consideration stage, quality becomes even more crucial. This is where you start addressing specific needs and pain points, showcasing your product's benefits in detail.

- **Content Types:** Case studies, product demos, FAQs, knowledge bases, tutorials, subject-matter expert videos.
- **Strategy:** Focus on creating high-quality, informative content that helps prospects evaluate your product or service. Use testimonials and case studies to build trust and credibility.

- **Example:** A detailed product demo video that explains the features and benefits of your product, hosted on your website and shared through email campaigns.

- **Focus—Value and Product Features:** Highlight the benefits and features of your product in detail.

Stage 4: Action

In the Action stage, the goal is to convert leads into customers. Here the content should be of the highest quality, addressing any final objections and providing a clear call to action.

- **Content Types:** Landing pages with strong CTAs, customer testimonials, discounts and promotions, trials, and samples.

- **Strategy:** Use persuasive, high-quality content to encourage conversions. Highlight success stories and provide detailed guidance on what happens after the purchase.

- **Example:** A customer testimonial video featuring success stories from clients, emphasizing the results achieved and the positive impact of your product.

- **Focus—Highest-Quality Content:** Provide the best content to encourage the final purchase decision.

Stage 5: Loyalty

After the purchase, maintaining customer loyalty is crucial. Content here should focus on ensuring customer satisfaction and encouraging repeat business.

- **Content Types:** Exclusive customer content, how-tos, community building (shared success stories).

- **Strategy:** Provide valuable content that supports the customer's ongoing use of your product. Share success stories and foster a community around your brand.

- **Example:** An exclusive webinar for customers showcasing advanced features of your product coupled with a Q&A session to address any issues.

- **Focus—Community and Continued Value:** Build a strong community and provide ongoing value to retain customers.

* * *

By aligning your content strategy with the QvQ Content Funnel, you can ensure that your marketing efforts are targeted, effective, and efficient at every stage of the customer journey. This approach enhances engagement and also drives higher conversion rates while fostering customer loyalty. It also gives direction on how to manage your content creation budget.

Figure 5.2 shows how certain types of content align with the sales funnel.

Buyer Stage	Content Types
Awareness	• Videos (more short than long form) • Blog Articles • Social Media Posts • Infographics
Interest	• Videos (more long than short form) • Podcasts • Newsletters • Webinars
Consideration	• Case Studies and Research • Product Demonstrations • FAQs and Knowledge Bases • Tutorials and Subject Matter Expert Video
Action	• Landing Pages with Strong CTAs • Customer Testimonials • Discounts and Promotions • Trials and Samples
Loyalty	• Exclusive Customer Content • Community Building (Shared Success Stories)

Figure 5.2 How content aligns with the sales funnel

This content marketing strategy provides Sales with a continuous stream of touchpoints to engage with prospects without being intrusive.

It keeps the prospect engaged and moving along the sales funnel, all the while being nurtured with valuable information.

Make sure that this sales funnel content alignment strategy is shared with your Sales team. For Sales, embracing content marketing means enhancing their toolbox with an array of resources that help in closing deals and also assist in building long-term relationships. The alignment between content marketing and Sales is a partnership that empowers Sales to be more effective, more empathetic, and more successful in converting leads to loyal customers.

Expert Insight—Joe Pulizzi

Joe Pulizzi is a seasoned entrepreneur and a pioneer in content marketing. He founded the Content Marketing Institute, which grew into the top global resource for content marketing education and training, and sold it to UBM in 2016. With his experience in building and selling several content businesses, Joe has unique insights on creating content that effectively supports sales strategies:

If you are only focused on the short term all the time, that is never a place that a salesperson wants to be. You know that a proper sales cycle takes time. When you first meet somebody, you don't expect to get the sale that day. And if you do, then you're in the wrong business. What you want to do is build relationships, and that database you built becomes a pre-customer database. These people will ultimately become customers, it just takes some time. Now, I get it—salespeople, they're on commission, and you want to see as much immediacy as you possibly can. But if you do this right, you'll set it up where you have people that are at every part of the sales cycle. And you'll see continuous sales, and you'll know that some people are not ready to buy and some are. Some people already bought, and there are opportunities for post-sales or additional sales to current customers. So I would just think about it more holistically from that standpoint.

Let's say you are a salesperson. You should work with Marketing and the Content Marketing team to make sure they're supplying you, on a weekly basis, answers to your biggest customer challenges, if you need help, if you can't come up with that yourself. So, what I want to do as a salesperson is make sure I'm listing all the customer challenges I get on an ongoing basis. I go into a sales call: What were the three top questions that I received? How am I answering those?

How could I answer those better? How could I integrate those answers into my regular communications with my customers? And a lot of salespeople don't do that. They're like, "Oh, okay. Well, I heard these problems here. I heard these over here in this call."

But then what I want to do is take that and integrate that back into everything I do—with my newsletters to my customers, in my communications on LinkedIn or threads or whatever you're doing, whatever you can commit to delivering on an ongoing basis, those solutions. What happens is that your Marketing team, they might not even know that. So, create a process where you're getting those questions and maybe some of those answers. Get that back to the people in Marketing so they can start embedding it and helping you.

There was a good case study from Xerox where the Content Marketing team was creating all sorts of content, and the Sales team didn't feel like it was adding any value. So the Xerox Marketing team ended up sending a weekly email to all the salespeople saying, "Look—here's all the content we have, but here are the top four things we think can help you in your job this week. Here's an e-book to this, solving this customer question. Here's a new report we have out. Here's a free webinar that you can send to clients." And I think that's very helpful because salespeople generally are not reading these emails. They don't even know what kind of content the Marketing team is coming up with.

But if the Marketing team can think, "Okay, this email is just going out to the salespeople. We're going to send it every Monday at 9 o'clock so the salespeople can embed that into their communications ongoing," I think it's really helpful.

In a lot of cases, the Content Marketing team isn't thinking, "Oh, my customer is also the Sales team."

Because what we want to do is make sure the Sales team actually uses all the content we're creating. Most salespeople don't. Most Marketing and Sales work separately, but there's a very easy solution to this problem: Solving that disconnect.

Data-Driven Decisions

One of the defining features of modern Marketing is the emphasis on data-driven decisions. It's not about designing flashy billboards or catchy jingles anymore. Instead, marketers now have a mind-bending amount of data to analyze—from website interactions, social media engagements, customer purchase histories, customer sentiment, industry trends, and even geographic movements. By leveraging data analytics, marketers can identify target audience segments, predict consumer behavior, customize messaging, and measure the success of campaigns in real time. Sales may not fully appreciate the depth of analysis involved in data-driven marketing, which is a crucial foundation for lead generation and nurturing.

Let's help Sales understand the extent of data used in marketing and the impact of Marketing's data on the Sales team by looking more deeply into several aspects of data-driven marketing.

1. Predictive Analytics for Lead Quality

Traditional lead generation might result in a mixed bag of potential clients, with Sales spending countless hours qualifying leads. Data-driven decisions in marketing allow for predictive analytics, where algorithms process past successes and client behavior to predict the likelihood of conversion. This means that Sales receives higher-quality leads that are better aligned with the product or service, thus saving time and improving conversion rates.

An important part of predicting lead quality is the practice of *lead scoring*. Lead scoring is an invaluable technique used within marketing automation platforms to rank and evaluate leads based on a multitude of criteria. These include aspects such as the prospect's interaction with the company's content, demographic information, and past purchase behavior. The concept aims to quantify how valuable each lead is, allowing Sales to prioritize their efforts accordingly.

Complementing the demographic approach in lead scoring is the intricate utilization of psychographics. Whereas demographics classify leads based on quantifiable attributes like age, occupation, or geographic location, psychographics involve the more subjective characteristics of individuals. Psychographics explore aspects like interests, values, attitudes, and lifestyle preferences. By understanding these nuances of a lead, Sales can craft messages and approach strategies that resonate on a deeply personal level.

The combination of demographics and psychographics creates a richer, more comprehensive profile of leads, thus enhancing the Sales team's ability to engage meaningfully and drive conversions. Knowing who the potential customers are and understanding what drives them allows Sales to connect in a manner that goes beyond surface-level statistics.

The process begins with the Marketing and Sales teams collaboratively identifying and weighing factors that signify a lead's likelihood of converting into a customer. This can encompass various touchpoints such as website visits, email engagements, social media interactions, industry details, job titles, and more. Additional company information such as company size, annual revenue, similar product use, and more can also be factored in. Using these predefined criteria, the marketing automation platform applies an algorithm that assigns points to each lead. The cumulative score for each lead is calculated and ranked, with higher scores reflecting leads that are more aligned with the company's ideal customer profile. It's essential to note that lead scoring is not a static process; scores continuously update as prospects engage with different touchpoints. Most platforms signify this fluctuation as a growing or shrinking number of points, stars, or even flame icons.

The integration of lead scoring into the customer relationship management (CRM) system offers substantial value. By surfacing this data into the CRM, Sales can quickly identify the most promising leads and focus on those with higher scores. This approach allows Sales to tailor their engagement strategies based on the factors contributing to a lead's score, ensuring personalized and effective communication. The alignment between Sales and Marketing is further enhanced as both teams work from the same scoring criteria, fostering a unified approach to engaging prospects. This scoring data aids in the optimization of Sales' time and resources, concentrating efforts on opportunities with the highest potential return.

It is important to first note that for lead scoring to be successful, it is critical that Sales has the dominant input on the scoring criteria. Even if the marketing automation platform manages the scoring, the scoring matrix should have buy-in from Sales and should be reviewed regularly to ensure that the scoring aligns with what truly defines a hot lead. Second, the scoring must be consistent across all teams and regions using the same system. A score number for one lead (100 points, for example) must mean the exact same thing/value for another lead. You don't want 100 points meaning "warm" for one lead and "hot" for another. This will result in the Sales team losing trust in the scoring system. If this is not managed through collaboration, Marketing may be seen as not understanding the Sales process, therefore eroding the relationship.

Lead scoring also feeds into enhanced analytics and reporting within the CRM, providing insights into trends, conversion rates, and the effectiveness of various marketing channels. These insights lead to more informed business decisions and allow continuous refinement of the scoring criteria based on actual sales performance.

By translating complex prospect interactions into a tangible score and making this information accessible in the CRM, organizations create a dynamic, aligned, and efficient lead management process. Lead scoring serves as a predictive tool that enriches Sales' strategies, ensures personalized engagement, promotes resource optimization, and contributes to a more effective sales operation.

2. Customer Segmentation for Tailored Engagement

Customer segmentation is the practice of dividing a company's customers into groups that reflect similarities in various ways, such as job title, age, gender, interests, spending habits, or behavior. Segmentation variables like these may catch your attention by not being politically correct. However, in business, you are considering and gathering these factors as data in order to drive decisions—not make judgments. You want to group people into the largest, most likely purchasers of your product.

These groups, or segments, are created based on specific characteristics that are relevant to a particular business, allowing Marketing teams to target these subsets of customers with communications that are much more personalized and relevant to their unique needs and preferences.

However, segmentation should go beyond categorization and dig more deeply into the layers of customer behaviors, preferences, and emotional triggers to craft a more personalized marketing strategy. Understanding customer behaviors is paramount as it involves recognizing patterns from purchase history, product usage, digital engagement, and response to previous marketing efforts. For instance, customers who regularly engage with eco-friendly products might reveal a segment that values sustainability.

Analyzing customer preferences further refines segmentation by identifying what resonates most with different individuals, drawn from factors like survey responses, feedback, or social media interactions. Recognizing these preferences enables Marketing to create personalized offerings and messages, such as targeting a segment that prefers online shopping with app-exclusive promotions.

Emotional triggers add nuance to this process, looking into the feelings and motivations that drive customer decisions. Techniques like sentiment analysis and in-depth interviews can uncover values, aspirations, fears, or desires that influence customer choices. This emotional understanding allows for the crafting of messages that connect on a deeper, more emotive level, like building trust with a segment that emphasizes security.

The fusion of these insights leads to the creation of specific customer personas—detailed and semi-fictional representations of ideal customers that encapsulate the defined segments. These personas guide the creation of personalized marketing messages, campaigns, and product recommendations, allowing marketing to move beyond generic strategies.

The personalization involved also consists of creating content that speaks to specific needs, preferences, and triggers, reflecting an understanding of the customer's identity and values. This continuous process of learning and targeting, coupled with ongoing refinement through monitoring and analyzing customer interactions, ensures that marketing messages remain relevant and effective.

By employing customer segmentation in this multifaceted way, Marketing can foster greater engagement and loyalty, optimizing resources, driving higher conversion rates, and strengthening the brand's relationship with its audience.

3. ROI Analysis for Optimized Investment

Understanding what marketing channels and strategies yield the best return on investment (ROI) is crucial for resource allocation. We need to grasp where investments in marketing strategies are garnering real value and how those insights can drive future decision-making.

ROI analysis for optimized investment takes a keen look at the conversion rates, lead quality, customer engagement, and revenue growth stemming from specific marketing initiatives. This analysis allows Marketing teams to pinpoint where their efforts are paying off and where they need to shift or intensify resources.

Sales teams, for their part, have to understand the importance of this data. The insights derived from ROI analysis represent a road map to greater sales success. These figures show which marketing channels are reaching the target audience, which messages are resonating, and where there's room for growth.

Imagine launching a targeted marketing campaign backed by rigorous data analysis. If this campaign results in higher lead conversion rates, you know you're on to something. Conversely, if a particular aspect of the campaign is underperforming, ROI analysis will highlight this, enabling real-time adjustments.

This is another opportunity for enhanced Sales-to-Marketing communication as well. While Marketing provides detailed ROI analysis, Sales must communicate their on-the-ground insights back to Marketing. What's working in real-life customer interactions? Where are potential customers falling out of the sales funnel? By working together, using ROI as a shared language, both teams can ensure that investments in marketing are being spent wisely.

Remember, ROI is more than a final report card; it's a continual learning process. Leveraging the insights from ROI analysis ensures that both Sales and Marketing are on the same page and working toward the same goals. It helps to make intelligent, informed decisions that align with the overarching strategy of the company. By consistently analyzing ROI, Sales and Marketing can optimize investments, align their efforts, and drive sustained growth in a way that is both efficient and effective.

It's important to note here, as I will in other areas of this book, that ROI is often a friction point between Marketing and Sales. Determining ROI from the Sales team can often be measured on a transactional basis: "We spend X on a sales encounter; we get a deal worth X amount of money." For Marketing, the touchpoints and efforts are spread across the entire base of potential and current customers. Most marketing efforts can be referred to as "the long game," and no single effort can be tied to any single deal.

This is the root of a major measurement flaw in most organizations. Measuring Marketing by the same timeline as that for Sales is a mistake. The best marketing campaigns and initiatives could take months to show results. To Sales, anything that takes months or a year might sound like a failure. But that's only when measured by the ruler that Sales is measured by. When your Sales team is measured by year, quarters, and halves, it may be hard for them to accept that Marketing's results, even highly successful ones, could take much longer to reveal an ROI.

4. Real-Time Feedback for Continuous Improvement

Data-driven decisions in marketing play a pivotal role in providing real-time feedback, enabling a fluid and dynamic approach to campaigns. This real-time assessment allows Marketing to immediately identify shifts in customer needs, the competitive landscape, or industry trends. By utilizing this continuous flow of information, they can tweak and enhance campaigns to align with these ever-changing parameters.

Sales, in turn, benefit significantly from this agility in Marketing. As campaigns are adjusted in real time, Sales is equipped with the most effective collateral and support. No longer is Sales forced to rely on outdated or irrelevant material; instead, they can be empowered with resources that directly respond to the current market pulse.

For example, if a new competitor enters the market with a unique selling proposition, Marketing can swiftly analyze this development through data-driven insights. By adjusting the messaging, positioning, or even the target audience in real time, Marketing ensures that Sales is not caught off guard. Instead, Sales is prepared with updated materials that can counter this new market challenge.

Similarly, if data reflects a sudden change in customer preferences or needs, Marketing can promptly alter the campaign to resonate with this shift. As a result, Sales is immediately supported with content and strategies that align with the fresh customer perspective, ensuring they don't struggle with a mismatched pitch.

The continuous feedback loop created by data-driven decisions fosters a nimble and responsive collaboration between Sales and Marketing. It removes the lag that often hampers adaptability, ensuring that both teams are in sync with the market's heartbeat. This synergy enhances the effectiveness of both Sales and Marketing while positioning the entire organization to seize opportunities and navigate challenges swiftly and precisely.

5. Alignment with Sales Goals and Metrics

Perhaps most convincingly, data-driven marketing can be tailored to align directly with sales goals and metrics, especially concerning the key performance indicators (KPIs) that we will discuss later. By working together, Sales can communicate what success looks like for them and Marketing can employ data to strategically drive toward those specific goals. Whether it's targeting a particular industry, increasing upsells, or expanding into new territories, data-driven marketing supports Sales in a way that's synergistic and goal-oriented.

* * *

In essence, data-driven decisions made by Marketing are not an isolated, abstract concept. They form the backbone of a collaborative and strategic partnership with Sales, enhancing efficiency, personalizing engagement, optimizing investment, enabling agility, and aligning with common goals. Sales professionals who embrace and understand the value of data-driven marketing are able to leverage a potent tool that elevates their success and sets the stage for continued growth and profitability.

Personalization and Customer Experience

Personalization, in the context of Sales and Marketing, goes far beyond dropping a prospect's first name into an email greeting. It's about delivering an experience that resonates with the individual needs, preferences, and behaviors of each customer or prospect. When Marketing works to provide a personalized experience to prospective customers, it should be seen as a tool that Sales can also use as a finely tuned approach that can drive deeper engagement and ultimately close more deals. The customers need to feel like you are selling directly to them, and only them, throughout their buying journey.

Imagine trying to sell a suit to a customer. If you know nothing about the customer, you might show them every suit in the store, hoping one catches their eye. But if you know the customer's size, favorite color, the event they're shopping for, and their budget, you'd be able to pick out the perfect options that meet their needs. That's personalization.

Due to the noise received by prospects from multiple brands trying to get their attention, personalization is a necessity. Prospects and customers expect companies to understand their unique requirements. This is why generic pitches often fall flat. By leveraging data and insights, Marketing can create tailored experiences that speak directly to an individual's specific situation. This can be a game-changer for Sales.

Here are some reasons why:

> **Understanding Customer Behavior:** By analyzing how customers interact with content, products, or services, Sales can gain insights into what resonates with individual prospects. Are they

clicking on articles about a specific product feature? Are they watching videos related to a particular use case? Are they asking for demonstrations of specific products or solutions? Understanding these behaviors allows Sales to tailor their approach, focusing on what matters most to each prospect.

Tailoring Content and Communication: Personalization enables Sales to provide relevant content at the right time. This might include sending a prospect a case study that aligns with the prospect's industry or sharing a video that addresses a specific challenge the prospect is facing. For perfect timing, automation can be used to trigger the sending of this content based on the customer's actions. In other words, if the person does *this*, then we send the person *that*. This tailored content helps to build rapport and also moves the prospect closer to making a buying decision.

Enhancing Customer Experience: Personalized interactions make customers feel understood and valued. By acknowledging a prospect's unique needs and preferences, Sales can build trust and deepen the relationship. This doesn't mean plugging the prospect's name into an email template you send to every person; it means understanding the prospect's pain points, goals, and desires, and then reflecting that understanding in every interaction.

Streamlining the Sales Process: Through personalization, Sales can provide the right information, answer the right questions, and address the right objections, all at the right time. This efficiency means less time wasted on irrelevant details and more time focused on what will drive the sale to close.

> *Caution:* This is where salespeople like to automate the sales process. They adopt tactics taught by a sales guru and begin using templated outreach methods. The big problem with this is that the prospect is getting targeted by multiple companies, and all their Sales teams are using the same templates. The result is that the prospect sees an email or outreach tactic like yours multiple times a day. While you, the salesperson, think

what you are doing is unique, your emails and direct messages are just like the dozens of other spammy communications that the prospect received that day.

Long-Term Engagement: When done correctly, personalization is not a one-time event. It's a continuous process that helps in nurturing long-term relationships. Post-sale, personalization can be used to deliver customized support, special offers, and content that encourages repeat business and brand loyalty. This is one of those intersection points where Sales benefits greatly from having access to Marketing data. The more a salesperson knows about the marketing data, the more that person knows the customer.

When Marketing aligns with Sales to provide personalization of the message to the customer, without doubt, a powerful strategy emerges for Sales. It empowers salespeople to be more precise, more responsive, and more successful in connecting with prospects on a deeper level. It enables the insertion of understanding, empathy, and relevance into every interaction. It can create an experience as unique as the individual you're speaking to.

Social Media and Influencer Marketing

Marketing's role in social media goes beyond just posting for likes and views. It's about a carefully planned strategy that supports Sales. By monitoring social media conversations, we gain insights into how our brand is perceived. This helps us manage our reputation proactively.

Social listening also lets us understand customer sentiment and feedback on our products. This means Sales can present a brand that aligns well with our audience and use real-time information to guide their conversations with prospects.

Engaging on social media and working with influencers will extend our brand's reach and credibility. This helps warm prospects up to the sales approach, driving lead generation. As a result, Sales gets prospects who are already interested.

By analyzing social media metrics, Marketing can continuously improve campaigns and support Sales with updated strategies. This use of social media provides tangible value for Sales, giving them insights that are important in a market where customers control the information they consume.

Customer opinions and trends change rapidly. When Sales teams are backed by Marketing's effective use of social media, they are better positioned for success.

With social media being just one of the facets of marketing, the *role* of Marketing has expanded and evolved significantly, marked by the need for strategic planning, data analysis, content creation, personalization, and the use of new platforms and technologies. As we mentioned earlier, Sales must value and view Marketing as a part of the Revenue team—not as a less important administrative role designed to serve them. One of the strongest reasons for this is the shifts in the customer journey.

It's essential that Sales recognize these shifts and understand the depth of modern Marketing's role so both teams can work together more effectively toward shared objectives. Remember, Marketing is more than just "making things look pretty." The essence of modern Marketing is about delivering the right message to the right person at the right time through the right channel—and social media continues to be a primary channel for the foreseeable future.

Expert Insight—Todd Ervin

Todd Ervin serves as principal for Cortado Group, leading client engagements as an interim chief marketing officer. His previous roles include Vice President of Marketing for Primo Water Corporation, Associate Vice President at North Highland, and Director of Marketing and Communications for Georgia Tech's Scheller College of Business. Additionally, Ervin's career spans leadership positions with Omnicom's Cultur8, Turner, NASCAR, and Sprint, in addition to service with the U.S. Army as an Apache attack helicopter pilot.

Todd shares a case from his time at Primo Water (water.com) where Marketing, Sales, and leadership worked together to fine-tune their system for a full-funnel approach to converting more customers:

> It was an instant clue that we—and not just Primo, but the whole industry—had no awareness at the top of the funnel that water delivery was even a thing. So it was a very quick calculation to say, "Guys, we haven't been doing anything at the top of the funnel. The customers that we get are in love with us. So how do we get the message out there and shift some of our marketing budget smartly to start some more top-of-the-funnel marketing?" And the thing I had to do from an approach perspective is, I had to get leadership. I had to get the CEO on board with this. I had to get CRO on board, because people get nervous when you start trying to move things that work. What I was able to explain to them is, "I'm going to shift a little bit of budget so that we can prove out the model that top-of-the-funnel content creation is what's needed in top of the funnel. Content will get more people into the funnel. Our conversion rates at the bottom of the funnel are great, but I'm not just going to take this big chunk of the budget and shift it and miss the numbers that we have been making."

You have to go about it with this case of proving it out. And again, proving it out also gets back to the systems. You have to have the right systems in place to track your marketing campaign so that now you can show the CEO this nice, pretty dashboard that says, "This is what we got from this campaign and here's how we were able to track these customers all the way through to conversion coming in off these awareness campaigns we had out in the market." So, you've got to have the tools that are collecting the data and analytics for you that allow you to visualize that data for the rest of the C-suite and the leadership team.

Then that's how you justify adding to your marketing budget to get more for the top of the funnel. Now they can see it, and you put numbers behind it, and you tie it back to revenue. Because in the C-suite, marketing speak like "impressions" and "likes" and all that . . . they don't care. [There is a problem] if you can't talk about how that's going to tie to a revenue number. I use an ROI calculator that says, "I know my conversion rates." I don't even talk to them about the impressions, but this is how I calculate it: If I get X number of impressions at the top, it's going to mean this many marketing-identified leads. They're going to lead to this many marketing-qualified leads and this many sales-accepted leads. Which, per our average revenue per customer or per sale, is going to mean this much in revenue if we do it this way. You have to be able to back it up with data and numbers and try to tie it back to ROI in order for a marketer to get the budget that's needed to do that awareness.

A lot of marketers go in and say, "I'm going to build all this great content. We're going to blast today"—and it's not tied back to the ICP (ideal customer profile) or the buyer persona either. They're going to take this shotgun blast approach, which is going to waste a lot of money. It still has to be very targeted, but again, targeted to a bit of a broader audience. So now, at the top of the funnel, instead of just launching campaigns to my A and B ICPs, I'm starting to include the Cs in there. And maybe some Ds as you rank ICPs. But you're expanding that for top of the funnel. It's going to cost you a little bit more money. But at the end of the day you're going to get more of the right people.

The Role of Sales—Sorry, the Customer Is in Charge

We mentioned earlier that the customer journey is almost completely in the customer's hands. This has had a profound impact on the role of Sales. For this reason, it is equally important that Marketing understand the persisting and important role of Sales despite the fact that customers choose to engage with Sales later in the customer journey.

At one time, salespeople were the gatekeepers of information. Customers could only gain deep knowledge about a product or service if they interacted with Sales. From the historical traveling salesman to the "Get a Demo" button of a website, Sales has always attempted to leverage their access to product information.

Today Sales can no longer be the gatekeeper of information. They must now act as interpreters, guides, and relationship builders. They serve as the human touch in a highly digitized marketplace, translating general marketing messages into specific solutions that resonate with individual customers. This shift in responsibility has turned Sales into a critical pivot point where prospects' interests are turned into commitments, creating a connection that transcends data alone.

The evolving role of Sales in today's customer-driven digital journey is marked by several key functions that extend far beyond traditional selling.

Humanizing the Brand Experience

People buy from people. Whether it's the salesperson or the influencer, humanizing the brand experience is crucial for bringing a brand to life in the minds and hearts of customers. Sales must take the lead in this process by becoming the living face of the brand, going beyond automated systems to build genuine connections.

To start, salespeople need to practice empathy. Actively engaging with customers and seeking to understand the individual behind the purchase is essential. This involves listening to concerns, asking thoughtful questions, and grasping each customer's unique situation. A personalized approach demonstrates to customers that their opinions and needs are valued.

Focusing on building enduring relationships through personalized interactions is of high value. Following up, providing ongoing support, and committing to customer satisfaction are essential steps. This relationship-building process fosters trust, converting customers into loyal advocates.

Also essential for enhancing the customer experience are personal touchpoints such as well-timed calls, thoughtful emails, and face-to-face meetings. These interactions add depth to the customer journey, which may feel impersonal without them.

The humanized brand experience leads to tangible business outcomes. Customers who feel cared for and understood are more likely to repeat business, refer others, and become vocal brand champions. In a competitive market, the ability to create emotional connections can be a vital differentiator.

Salespeople also play a role as educators and guides. They facilitate individual sales and contribute to a broader perception of the brand as accessible, responsive, and customer-centric. Personalizing and humanizing interactions elevate the brand, enrich the customer experience, and drive long-term success. Striving to make the brand relatable, Sales teams change the brand into something real and engaging. This approach builds trust, engagement, and loyalty, laying the foundation for a lasting brand connection.

Providing Insights for Marketing Strategy

As we discussed in the Communications chapters, providing insights for marketing strategy is a central component of Sales and Marketing collaboration. Salespeople engage with customers face-to-face through calls, meetings, and various customer touchpoints. During these engagements, they hear the questions customers are asking, sense their hesitations, and learn about their particular needs and aspirations. These aren't abstract data points on a spreadsheet; they're real-world insights, offering a glimpse into the minds and hearts of the customers.

This information isn't anecdotal. When captured and shared systematically, these insights become a reservoir of intelligence that can guide the Marketing department's strategies and tactics. Salespeople's experiences can reveal the gaps in understanding that customers might have, the particular language they use, or the specific problems they are trying to solve. They may also uncover new trends or shifts in customer behavior that haven't yet been identified through other channels.

Salespeople's understanding of customer objections, for instance, can help Marketing craft content that preemptively addresses these concerns or reshape product messaging to better align with customer needs. Their insight into what resonates with customers can help Marketing prioritize efforts, concentrating resources on channels, messages, or offers that have proved to engage the target audience. This real-time feedback loop ensures that marketing strategies are not built on assumptions or outdated data but are continually refined to mirror the evolving customer landscape.

Furthermore, the Sales team's role as the eyes and ears of the company extends beyond influencing marketing efforts. By being in constant dialogue with customers, they offer an early warning system for potential challenges, a source of inspiration for innovation, and a gauge for measuring customer satisfaction. They become the connection between the customer and the company, helping to create a culture that values customer needs and feedback. This intelligence and flow of information also ensures that Marketing doesn't operate in a vacuum and is aligned with the realities on the ground, making it more responsive, agile, and effective.

Simply put, when a salesperson interacts with customers, their ability to listen, interpret, and communicate these experiences back to Marketing can ensure that the organization remains tuned in to its most crucial stakeholder—the customer. This alignment helps build a brand that doesn't just promote products but truly responds to customers with understanding, accuracy, and relevance.

Creating Tailored Solutions

"Creating tailored solutions" may sound like a catchphrase for salespeople, but it can actually be a crucial aspect of their role in a customer-centric environment. Unlike a predefined online purchase path, which may not account for the nuances of individual needs, salespeople possess the agility to craft solutions that align exactly with a particular customer's unique situation. This involves understanding the distinct challenges, desires, and preferences that shape a customer's choice—and then offering a responsive, customized approach to solve the customer's problem.

A tailored solution should be designed to go beyond only offering a product or service. It involves a closer look into the customer's context, analyzing the factors that influence the customer's decisions and identifying the underlying problems that need solving. Salespeople are skilled in navigating these complexities, engaging in conversations that unearth the core issues, and then developing bespoke offerings that resonate with those specific needs.

This adaptive approach adds a layer of personalization that standard online options often lack. It goes beyond selling a product. It should involve sculpting a package or service that mirrors the customer's expectations and solves the customer's particular problems. This careful crafting requires a blend of empathy, creativity, and strategic thinking, qualities that set salespeople apart in a business where automated purchasing isn't standard.

Shaping offers or services to bring tangible value to the customer experience enhances satisfaction and loyalty. It signals to customers that they're more than another number in a database; they are valued individuals whose unique needs matter. This personal connection often leads to higher conversion rates, as customers recognize the effort and attention devoted to serving them. They appreciate the minimized friction between what's offered and what they actually need, which brings trust and a sense of partnership that encourages ongoing engagement with the brand.

Especially in markets saturated with options, the salesperson's capacity to create tailored solutions sets a brand apart. It's a clear sign of customer-centric thinking, a philosophy that recognizes the individuality of each customer and strives to meet them where they are. This practice wins hearts, minds, and wallets, creating stronger relationships with your customers that are designed to last and grow.

Becoming the Trusted Advisor

The salesperson's role should be to educate and guide the customer toward an action that benefits them both. While the internet has democratized access to data about products and services, this abundance can often overwhelm rather than clarify. Customers may find themselves tangled in options, contradictory advice, or technical jargon that doesn't connect with their unique needs. Salespeople should have the experience to translate this complex information into terms that resonate with the customer's specific circumstances.

By engaging in thoughtful conversations, salespeople can uncover the underlying goals and challenges the customer faces, crafting personalized solutions that align with those objectives. This approach allows the salesperson to become a trusted advisor. Once in this position, a salesperson can initiate a consultative dialogue to assist customers in navigating through the noise, sorting out options, and linking products and services to the customer's situation. This link is the desired action. In order to make that action happen, the customers need to be influenced by someone with real experience and with the authority to lead them in the right direction. This is visualized in Figure 5.3.

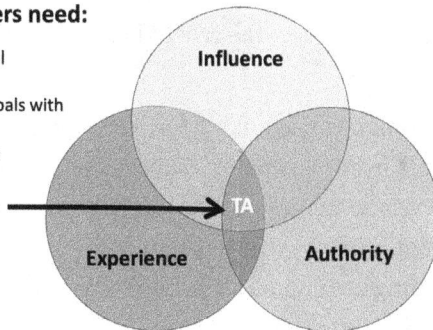

To create Action, customers need:

- **Influence** by someone with real
- **Experience** relatable to their goals with
- **Authority** to lead in a direction

⩵ Trusted Advisor

Influence

Experience

Authority

TA

Figure 5.3

93

Guiding customers to make informed and confident decisions, Sales serves as a compass, influencing customers toward the right solutions while providing reassurance. This guidance builds trust and sets the stage for a collaborative and enduring relationship. Customers appreciate it when their Sales contact—the salesperson—brings added value through their insights, empathy, experience, and dedication to customer success. This gives the salesperson the authority to be worthy of the customer's consideration. At this point, the customer views the salesperson not as a vendor but as a partner; an ally who understands and is invested in the customer's achievements.

The transition from gatekeeper to influencer to trusted advisor reflects a profound change in the salesperson's function. It acknowledges the complexity of modern buying processes and the value of human insight in an increasingly digital landscape. Wisdom, context, and personalized attention remain highly sought-after commodities, ones that a skilled salesperson can offer to stand out and foster meaningful connections with customers.

Nurturing Long-Term Relationships

Nurturing a long-term relationship means going beyond closing a sale. It represents a core part of a salesperson's responsibilities and impact. Salespeople should understand that the customer journey doesn't end with a signed contract or completed transaction. Instead, they engage in continuous follow-up, regular check-ins, and consistent support, solidifying their role as the trusted advisors we mentioned earlier—not just order takers.

By remaining available for future needs and demonstrating genuine interest in the customer's success, salespeople convey the message that their relationship with the customer is not transactional, but transformational. They actively participate in the customer's ongoing journey, providing insights, advice, and solutions that align with changing needs and priorities.

These continuous touchpoints ensure that customers feel valued and cared for well after a purchase. They also lay the foundation for a mutually beneficial partnership. Such a relationship transcends the traditional buyer-seller dynamic and evolves into a collaboration based on trust, understanding, and shared goals.

This nurturing approach pays off in tangible ways, including ongoing loyalty, repeat business, and positive word-of-mouth referrals. But, perhaps more importantly, it embodies a philosophy of customer-centricity, where the salesperson's success is intertwined with the customer's satisfaction and growth. In this model, the role of Sales is not a one-time event. It's an ongoing process that recognizes the ever-evolving nature of customer needs and responds with empathy, engagement, and expertise.

Maintaining Customer Relationship Data

The role of Sales in maintaining customer data within the CRM is critical for cohesion with Marketing, and more importantly, it plays an important role in business operations as a whole. By meticulously keeping track of customer interactions, preferences, opportunity details, and deal information, Sales lays the foundation for accurate reporting and analysis. This is why what might be seen as tedious data entry or administrative work is, in reality, a strategic function that drives forecasting, informs future strategies, and shapes decision-making processes.

The information that Sales captures and curates within the CRM becomes the lifeblood of the organization's ability to understand its customers and predict their behavior. Regularly refreshing this data ensures that it remains relevant and actionable, facilitating timely responses and targeted strategies. When done with care and consistency, the effort Salespeople puts into managing data transforms the CRM from being simply an information repository to being a dynamic tool that enhances understanding, sharpens focus, and contributes to the company's agility in a competitive marketplace.

In summary, the maturity of Sales into a strategic, relationship-oriented, customer-centric function emphasizes the need for alignment with Marketing. Customers controlling their own journey, with access to vast information, are met by salespeople who need to adapt by weaving empathy, intelligence, customization, education, and technology-assisted personalization into their interactions. Sales, when fully involved in the customer journey, can become indispensable in turning prospects into satisfied customers.

This evolution in Sales requires alignment with Marketing to create a unified customer experience. Sales guides customers personally, providing education and customized solutions, while Marketing shapes the broader strategy by leveraging insights and feedback from Sales. Together, they create tailored messages and offers that resonate on a personal level.

The alignment between Sales and Marketing is a connection between functions and a strategic partnership. They work collaboratively, understanding each other's roles and contributions, to build a brand that stands out, both for its products and for its customer-centric approach. Sales is a vital component of a cohesive Marketing strategy.

In essence, the alignment between Sales and Marketing strengthens the entire business framework. Sales' strategic, relationship-building, customer-centric approach combined with Marketing's data-driven insights creates an integrated, synergistic strategy that fosters authentic connections and brand loyalty. Beyond tactics, this alignment begins to create the Revenue team that all companies dream of.

Chapter 6

Sharing Key Performance Indicators

The Importance of Shared KPIs

Imagine a team sport where the players are divided into two groups: one for attacking and one for defending. If the attacking group's performance is measured by how many goals they score, and the defending group's success is measured by how many goals they prevent, you have two separate key performance indicators (KPIs). However, these separate measurements viewed one at a time will not accurately reflect or predict the overall performance of the team. For example, the defending group could prevent all goals against them, thus achieving their KPI, while the attacking group fails to score, missing their KPI. Evaluating them separately leads to a skewed perspective where one part appears successful, even though the team as a whole doesn't win the game.

The same principle applies to Sales and Marketing within a business. If Sales is measured only by the number of deals created or closed in a specific time period and Marketing is measured solely by leads generated in that same period, their individual successes or failures may not align with the overall goals of the company. Imagine this common scenario: What if a unified Sales and Marketing team increased the qualified pipeline for large deals by 80% in the first quarter? And this was done through marketing campaigns that ignited the existing customer base regarding a new offering. The Sales team then activates efforts to close the bigger deals.

Keep in mind the scenario here—existing customers and bigger deals requiring a longer sales negotiation. The result would be no new leads reported from Marketing and no closed deals reported from Sales . . . for that period. I repeat, "For that period." Individually, each team could be viewed as missing or failing their KPIs. This reveals a misalignment between strategy measurement and time frame.

Let's go a step further to assume you understand and correct for the error made of measuring by the wrong time frame. You instead look at the end of the year to measure each individual team. Did Marketing fail because they did not create enough net new leads? If net new leads were the KPI, this would count as a failure. Marketing was very successful, just not by the erroneous KPI of "*new* leads."

A similar error could happen if the Sales team was measured by quarter. These bigger deals could break the normal sales cycle; if those measuring Sales don't realize this, they could make the error of punishing the Sales team with accusations of not meeting quarterly KPIs.

By sharing KPIs and aligning their measurements in terms of number, value, and time frame, Sales and Marketing can ensure that they are working together toward the same objectives. This unified and cohesive approach allows both teams to understand how their efforts contribute to the broader success of the business, fostering collaboration and ensuring that individual achievements translate into collective victories.

I'll wrap up the sports analogy here by stating that the playing field for your Sales and Marketing members is the funnel. Not the sales funnel, not the marketing funnel, but a unified sales and marketing funnel—better referred to as a revenue funnel. There is only one funnel, and both parts of your team are working to move prospective customers down and out of the bottom.

Some don't like the idea of the funnel because it implies that leads come into the top of the funnel and either evaporate along the way or travel directly to the bottom to become new customers. The reality is that you can affect prospects before they even enter the funnel. Then, as you can see in Figure 6.1, once they enter, prospects can bounce back out of the top of the funnel, exit through the sides of the funnel, return to the top, and reenter through the sides (multiple times) before, hopefully, reaching the bottom. They can even pick up a few buying group members along the way. No matter how much we try to plan a customer journey, this is what a true funnel looks like—because it is the customer's journey, not ours. The customers are the captains now.

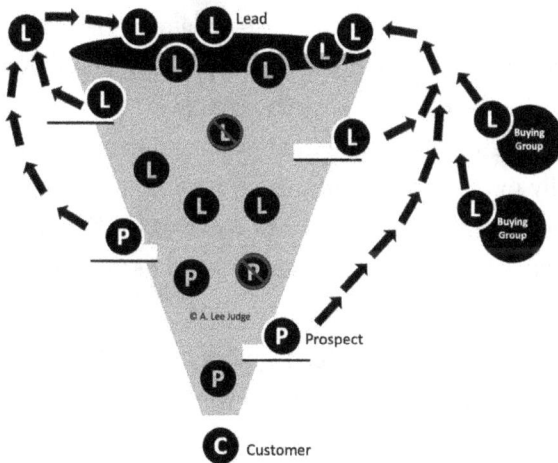

Figure 6.1 What funnel behavior really looks like

Building Shared KPIs

So how and where do we measure our efforts to move prospects through that funnel? While it is necessary for Marketing to have their KPIs, and individual Sales team members can have their KPIs, it is vital that the two teams share KPIs if they are to successfully create adequate revenue.

Here are examples of KPIs that can and should be shared between Sales and Marketing.

Lead Conversion Rate

Both Sales and Marketing should be concerned with how many leads are converted into customers. Even if Marketing generates the leads, they must continuously work with Sales to close the deal. Even after an initial deal is closed by Sales, keeping the prospects in the funnel and convincing them to stay in contact with Sales and buy again is an integral part of Marketing's job as well. By sharing this KPI, both teams can align their strategies to ensure that leads don't just get generated but are of the quality and type that are more likely to convert into a customer—and then a repeat customer.

This must not be confused with the idea of a "marketing conversion." By definition, this is when unknown people complete a form and identify themselves. In other words, these people convert from unknown to known. This is important because we must find new people and identify them individually in order to communicate with them. However, this definition doesn't carry any weight in the Sales world because, at this point, we don't know if this marketing conversion has any chance of becoming a sales conversion.

In terms of measuring the lead conversion rate as a KPI, we want to understand how many of the people who identify themselves become viable prospects and then become actual customers.

For Sales, the lead conversion rate serves as a yardstick for both the quality of the leads and the effectiveness of the sales process. If you have a high rate of conversion, it tells you that Marketing is sending you the right kind of fuel for your engine. It shows the leads are not just names but prospects genuinely interested in your products with the intent to buy. On the flip side, if the conversion rate is low, it could be a prompt to dig deeper, collaborate with Marketing, and understand if the problem lies in the lead quality (the most common accusation), the sales tactics (the most common oversight), or perhaps a combination of both. No matter the outcome, it allows Sales to refine their approach and focus their energy where it is most likely to yield results.

For Marketing, a shared focus on the lead conversion rate keeps the team aligned with the end goal—not only attracting eyeballs but also nurturing these prospects through a journey that culminates in a sale. It offers a reality check; if leads aren't converting, it's time to reevaluate the messaging, targeting, or even the channels used for lead generation. It acts as a critical feedback loop for improving future marketing campaigns and understanding what resonates with the target audience. Essentially, sharing this KPI with Sales ensures that Marketing is not operating in a vacuum and is intricately linked to actual business outcomes.

Marketing Qualified Leads

I addressed the lead conversion rate first in order to properly address the elephant in the room—the marketing qualified lead, or MQL. This is *not* a shared KPI; however, for the purpose of completing the conversation, we must address it.

An MQL is a marketing performance indicator to show how many leads meet Marketing's criteria of worthiness to pass on to Sales. *Caution:* This is where the Marketing team messes up the most and can absolutely lose the respect of Sales. If they operate in a vacuum and don't define their criteria based on what Sales is looking for, the MQLs will mean nothing to the business.

If your team doesn't understand the points made in the Communication chapters of this book, they will likely be set up for an "MQL fail." Make sure the MQL criteria are aligned with and respond to the lead conversion rate. If Marketing is calling leads "qualified" and yet they never convert . . . they were not actually qualified in the first place.

Regarding the lead conversion rate, it is popular to calculate this number based on the total number of leads generated. However, to be more specific and avoid including fluff and trash leads in your metrics, I would advise that you calculate this number starting with only marketing qualified leads—thus an MQL conversion rate.

The calculation looks more accurately like this:

$$\text{MQL Conversion Rate} = \frac{\text{Number of Closed Sales from MQLs}}{\text{Total Number of MQLs Generated}} \times 100$$

Sales Qualification Rate

A sales-qualified lead, or SQL, is a lead that has progressed from Marketing to Sales and the salesperson sees the lead as qualified to pursue into an opportunity. You want to understand the rate of leads handed to Sales, which Sales deems being qualified enough to consider an opportunity. This is the sales qualification rate. It is the percentage of leads that move from being just a qualified lead to a qualified sales opportunity. This transition usually happens after a series of interactions or engagements where the Sales team assesses the lead's fit and intent. In essence, it answers the question, "How many of our leads (or prospects) are ready for a deeper sales conversation?" It's an invaluable KPI that provides a direct line of sight into the quality of leads generated and the effectiveness of the initial stages of the sales process.

It's important to note that some CRMs, such as Salesforce, consider a person a lead until Sales accepts the lead and converts the lead into a prospect (technically, Salesforce calls prospects "contacts"). Then, when this prospect reaches the stage of being attached to an opportunity, we have a sales qualification. These terms will vary per CRM platform. The point to understand is that when Sales spots an opportunity, you have a sales qualification.

Mathematically, it can be calculated as follows:

$$\text{Sales Qualification Rate} = \frac{\text{Number of Qualified Sales Opportunities}}{\text{Total Number of LeadsGenerated}} \times 100$$

Importance to Sales: For Sales, the sales qualification rate is like a barometer for efficiency. Time is a precious resource for Sales; therefore, being able to quickly and accurately identify which leads are worth pursuing is important. A higher sales qualification rate usually indicates that the leads being received are well targeted and high quality, meaning sales reps can spend more time closing deals rather than sifting through unqualified leads. In a competitive environment where every moment counts, knowing you're investing time in leads that are more likely to convert can be a game-changer. It helps in resource allocation, aids in more accurate sales forecasting, and, ultimately, can be a key factor in achieving or exceeding revenue goals.

Importance to Marketing: From a Marketing standpoint, the sales qualification rate serves as a reality check for the lead generation efforts. If the rate is low, it's a signal to revisit the targeting parameters, messaging, or channels being used to attract leads. It can provoke essential questions such as, "Are we targeting the right audience?" or, "Is our messaging aligned with what our most qualified prospects care about?" A high sales qualification rate, conversely, validates the marketing strategy and offers tangible evidence that marketing efforts are generating the right kind of interest.

* * *

To summarize these three terms and their relationship—the lead conversion rate and sales qualification rate are integral KPIs that bridge the efforts of the Sales and Marketing teams. The lead conversion rate gauges the effectiveness of both departments in progressing initial leads into customers, serving as a mutual metric that reflects the quality of leads sourced by Marketing and the efficacy of Sales' closing strategies.

On the other hand, the sales qualification rate specifically measures the transition of leads into bona fide sales opportunities, offering insights into the lead vetting process and early-stage sales acumen.

Marketing qualified leads are a key Marketing KPI. Their impact on lead conversion shows the need for a strong relationship with Sales to ensure leads are ready for conversion, aligning with sales strategy and business goals.

Together, these KPIs form a feedback loop that enhances targeting, messaging, and the allocation of resources, which is crucial for achieving revenue goals and aligning the Sales and Marketing teams.

Customer Lifetime Value

We mentioned before how critical it is that customers complete a sales cycle and then become poised to buy again as ongoing customers. In addition to the value of their original purchase, as they continue to buy, this increases their customer lifetime value (CLTV). This is not to be confused with revenue per lead, which is usually a short-term metric useful for gauging the initial effectiveness of a particular marketing strategy. CLTV is a more long-term metric. It doesn't stop at considering the revenue generated from the customer's first purchase; it looks at the total revenue customers will generate throughout their entire relationship with the brand. By understanding CLTV, you're getting a fuller picture of customer value that takes into account repeat purchases, loyalty, and referrals.

Using CLTV as a shared KPI helps Sales and Marketing understand how much value a customer is expected to bring over the entire relationship. It's a reflection of both the quality of the leads that Marketing is attracting and the ability of a unified Sales and Marketing team to nurture and maintain that relationship.

Why CLTV Should Matter to Sales
Understanding Revenue Potential

Sales leaders are driven by revenue growth and CLTV provides a clear picture of the long-term value of each customer. Beyond the initial sales effort, understanding CLTV allows Sales to strategize and focus efforts on nurturing relationships that will pay dividends over time.

A Focus on Retention

Given that we are discussing the dividends from a customer over time, it is important that the Sales KPIs allow them to buy into the idea that there is value in keeping the customer long term. If they are only incentivized to get the customer but have no incentive to keep them, their KPIs may not actually support the company's long term revenue objectives. Sales leaders should motivate their teams to acquire customers and maintain relationships that build long-term loyalty and revenue stability.

Customizing Sales Strategies

By understanding CLTV, Sales teams can categorize customers based on their potential value and tailor their sales approach accordingly. High-value customers might receive more personalized attention, while others might be targeted with more automated, scale-driven methods. Just as lead scoring directs Sales to the most sales-ready prospects, knowing a customer's CLTV can guide them on which existing customers to direct their attention.

Why CLTV Should Matter to Marketers

Quality over Quantity

Marketing teams are under pressure to generate new leads, but understanding CLTV helps to prioritize quality over quantity. By aligning campaigns and content to attract customers with higher potential lifetime value, Marketing can contribute to more meaningful and profitable relationships.

I'll give you a very important warning here though. If you are in Marketing, you will be in a constant struggle between when to deliver quality and when to deliver quantity. In a perfect world, Marketing would be able to deliver a high volume of quality leads all the time. If that were the case, we would all be living in a business growth utopia. Unfortunately, this is not the case.

In regard to timing, the delivery of quantity or quality to the Sales team can be about as difficult as timing the stock market. However, working to deliver the *right kinds* of leads at the *right time* is at the core of what marketing is.

When you are asked to focus on quality, your quantity will drop. And rightfully so. Every lead won't be of quality, so the numbers delivered to Sales will naturally be lower. But beware . . . the moment Sales feels a crunch to work on more leads, Marketing will receive a demand for more quantity. If Marketing is already delivering quality, developing more leads out of thin air to produce a higher quantity will only open the door to less quality. And thus begins the battle of quality versus quantity. This is a never-ending battle, so consider it a cycle.

Targeting Resources Toward the Right Customers

Knowing the long-term value of a customer can greatly improve the way you allocate your marketing resources. Even after you acquire new customers, you must continue focusing your energies where they will yield the highest return.

Sales teams often have a granular understanding of which accounts are most valuable. They know who buys frequently, who makes the big orders, and who refers new business. This information is gold, but it's often hoarded in the Sales silo. Imagine the power of breaking down that wall. If Marketing could align their targeting and resource allocation based on customer value, then every email sent, ad displayed, and content campaign launched would become significantly more impactful.

Without understanding CLTV, Marketing could be shooting arrows in the dark, hoping one will hit a high-value target. You might be pushing high-cost campaigns toward customers who aren't worth the investment. You may be offering premium services to leads that are more of a one-and-done deal. That's inefficient and a colossal waste of resources.

So for the marketers looking to level up, incorporating CLTV into your strategy isn't optional; it's essential. This KPI ensures you're in lockstep with Sales, targeting not just any customer, but the right customer. With this understanding, you will know who's most likely to buy, stick around, bring in the most revenue, and become a brand advocate.

Understanding and leveraging CLTV is not an isolated task. It requires a concerted effort from both Sales and Marketing. Sales must provide ongoing insights into customer behavior, satisfaction, and potential growth, while Marketing must leverage this information to create compelling, targeted campaigns that resonate with different customer segments.

A practical collaboration might involve Sales identifying high-value customers who are ripe for upselling or cross-selling and Marketing creating tailored content or offers to support these efforts. Conversely, if CLTV analysis reveals a segment of customers that is declining in value, Marketing and Sales are now armed to work together to understand why. With this data, they can choose whether to stop pursuing that type of customer or create strategies for reengaging to retain those customers.

In essence, CLTV is a valuable data point that, when recognized correctly, serves to bridge the division between Sales and Marketing. It can be used as a unifying metric that aligns both teams around a shared goal: long-term, profitable customer relationships. It fosters a collaborative mindset where both Sales and Marketing leaders see beyond their immediate roles, recognizing the interconnected contributions they make to overall business success. The focus on CLTV can transform the Sales and Marketing dynamic from a disjointed and sometimes competitive relationship into a cooperative, value-driven partnership that benefits the entire organization.

* * *

As we close out this section on building shared KPIs, we focus on the importance of unifying Sales and Marketing with metrics that reflect their joint efforts. The lead conversion rate and sales qualification rate emerge as pivotal indicators, guiding both teams to cultivate and convert leads more effectively. Through these KPIs, Marketing strives to deliver leads that align with Sales' criteria, an endeavor quantified by MQLs and the MQL conversion rate.

This alignment ensures both departments collaborate effectively and stay attuned to sales cycles and customer retention. Establishing shared KPIs shows a commitment to synchronized growth and demonstrates the power of collective revenue goals.

Expert Insight—Aaron Hassen

Aaron Hassen is a veteran marketing executive with over 20 years of experience in B2B technology and growth marketing. Throughout his career he has held leadership positions at several emerging tech companies, consistently driving two to three times annual revenue growth through innovative strategies and data-driven approaches. Aaron's expertise spans the full spectrum of marketing disciplines, from digital advertising and content marketing to product positioning and go-to-market strategies, making him a sought-after leader in the B2B tech marketing space.

Having a clear view of Marketing's role and how it is viewed by Sales, Aaron shares his experience regarding a unified strategy and how that, in turn, impacts the customer:

It starts with a shared cause and vision. You have to know you're headed in the same direction and fighting for the same thing. That's the starting point.

So when you're trying to function as one team, one of the key points in doing that, as you have a unified strategy, is then to look across your buyer journey and see it as one experience. Not a marketing experience that turns into a sales experience that turns into a client success experience. The customer does not have three experiences. You do not want them having three experiences. They have one experience with your brand.

As Sales sees that it's one experience, they also begin to see how they can take part in top of the funnel activities. If we go to events together and Marketing prepares those events and sets promotions and campaigns, what role does [Sales] need to play in that so that they can get qualified opportunities to demo and close? And a big part of functioning as a team is a shared accountability, so qualified opportunities are something I would hold Marketing accountable for. Qualified meetings, win-losses even. Some marketers don't want to take responsibility for win-losses.

But if you're sending junk through the pipeline, is there a level of responsibility Marketing has to win-loss? I would say yes. But even beyond that: average sale value. If you do your job right, you qualify well, you communicate well on the front end, you set expectations well--you should see your average sale value go up. If you're building value in the brand, the average sales should go up. Your time to close should go down. And then overall lifetime value—if you build a brand that people really want to be a part of and be loyal to, you'll see an effect in lifetime value. And even if that's more of a client success factor, it's also a role and a place where Marketing can make an impact.

Again, I think shared cause and vision, shared strategy, functioning as one team, and having shared accountability—that's where you get true unification between Sales and Marketing and more of a balanced relationship: more equality across the two departments.

Chapter 7

Organization Culture and Structure

The Organization's View of Marketing

Organizations typically see the Marketing team as less important than Sales. After all, when we evaluate a company, we ask, "What are the sales?"—not "How successful is the marketing?" That's fair, but not effective. All businesses must focus on selling things in order to survive. Still, this doesn't mean that they have to focus disproportionately on the Sales team.

There is a famous quote by Desmond Tutu about mercy and justice. When I visualize it, I can't help but see it also as a Sales and Marketing metaphor. He wrote:

"There comes a point where we need to stop just pulling people out of the river. We need to go upstream and find out why they're falling in."

I visualize the river as the business's sales pipeline. Only in this case, you need people coming down the river. And when people stop coming down the river for Sales to pull out, a business must go upstream to see why no one is falling in!

Unfortunately for many businesses, as long as there are leads to pull out of the river they assume there will always be people automatically jumping in upstream. Without Marketing, however, this would not be the case.

While Marketing finds and filters new leads for a business to pursue, it also continuously corrals these leads through the entire sales cycle— making sure that they stay in the pipeline, maintain interest, become customers, and stay customers.

As we mentioned in earlier chapters, the role of the Marketing team is not simply to be promotion drivers or creative task-takers. Coming up with catchy text and beautifying presentations is not the primary purpose for a Marketing team. Marketing must be acknowledged as a key part of the revenue generation process.

The integral role of Marketing extends far beyond lead generation. It is the lifeblood of a business, and going back to the river metaphor, it keeps business flowing downstream. Yet for Marketing to truly propel a business forward, it must be nurtured by the very culture of the organization. A company's ethos should celebrate the creativity, strategic thinking, and analytical prowess that Marketing brings. This recognition should be embedded into the company's DNA, reflected in resource allocation and how successes are rewarded.

A culture that elevates the importance of Marketing encourages an environment where every team member understands the impact of a well-nurtured lead and the storytelling behind a brand's success. When a business invests financially in its Marketing strategies, it sends a clear message: Marketing is not a secondary function but a cornerstone of the organization's growth and sustainability.

This financial endorsement, paired with verbal reinforcement from leadership, fosters a sense of value and respect for the Marketing team's efforts. It empowers marketers to innovate, take calculated risks and strive for the exceptional, knowing that the organization appreciates the profound link between strong marketing initiatives and overall business success.

In essence, the cultural shift that supports Marketing in both word and investment is about securing the future of the business—not about giving the team a pat on the back. It's a recognition that though Sales may reel in the catch, Marketing ensures there's always a bountiful stream from which to fish. By intertwining financial commitment with cultural reverence for Marketing, a business doesn't just wait for leads to fall into the river—it actively nurtures the streams that feed it, ensuring a steady flow of opportunity and prosperity.

How Does Marketing Get Financial Endorsement?

There is one thing marketers do the most that hurts how they are viewed by the business world: reporting on vanity metrics that do not roll up into the bottom line. Marketers must show the short- and long-term value of their efforts such as the influence on customers that are brought in, the effectiveness of marketing channels, and the efficiency in using company resources to drive revenue.

Marketing teams often walk a tightrope between creative expression and financial justification. To secure a financial endorsement they must pivot their focus from vanity metrics, which, while easily quantifiable, offer little insight into the company's bottom line. Instead, they should anchor their reports in metrics that reflect the actual economic impact of their efforts. This means zooming in on customer conversions attributed directly to marketing efforts, dissecting the effectiveness of different channels, and revealing the strategic use of company resources.

To connect promotional activities with sales numbers in a manner that secures financial endorsement, Marketing teams must leverage technology that gives some hint of attribution. I say "hint" because attribution is not an exact science. These hints are shown by each customer's interaction with marketing efforts, which can be monitored at some level (depending on the customer journey), establishing a trail from the first engagement to the final sale.

Incorporating attribution modeling into the mix allows marketers to determine the value each marketing channel brings to the table. It means getting beyond hunches and guesses and utilizing data to substantiate the narrative that marketing strategies are not noise but essential parts of the overall business strategy.

Marketing Attribution—the Search for the Holy Grail

Analytics of customer touchpoint information should be the marketer's compass, guiding them from what may be an overwhelming amount of marketing data to actionable insights. These analytics are primarily derived from the capabilities of marketing automation platforms (MAPs) and customer relationship management (CRM) platforms. These allow marketers to capture a wealth of interaction data from the initial first-touch impression to the closing of a sale. Reports generated from this data should clearly tie specific marketing endeavors to spikes in sales, giving credit where it's due. This evidence will speak volumes when it comes time for financial discussions.

Unfortunately, while there are many ways to measure marketing attribution, there is no single perfect way of determining what actions in marketing can be attributed to a final sale. When the marketing process became more digital and we were given the gift of tracking clicks and digital interactions, the thought was that we would be able to easily guide the customer journey and track the customer's steps along the way.

However, two fundamental shifts unraveled our hopes of this perfect world of marketing attribution. First, we realized that the customer owned the journey. It is the customer's journey, not ours. We could not determine what the customer saw first, what the customer interacted with, or what precisely triggered a buying decision. This revealed a major flaw in digital tracking. Not only did we have trouble figuring out what effort touched the customers in the first place; we also didn't know what impressions or conversations they had about our company when they were offline.

Then, as major companies like Google and Apple amassed significant customer journey data on users, growing privacy concerns among consumers led to a pushback. This, in turn, led to actions diminishing the reliance on browser cookies as a tracking tool.

To understand how marketing attribution works (and doesn't), let's first lay down a basic understanding of its concepts and three primary types.

Marketing attribution is the analytical practice of determining which marketing tactics are contributing to sales or conversions. Different types of attribution models help marketers understand the value of the various customer touchpoints that lead to a conversion.

Here are the three attribution types that are most often sought after:

1. **First-Touch Attribution:** This model credits the first customer interaction for any subsequent sale or conversion. For example, if a customer's first interaction with a brand is clicking on a PPC (pay per click) ad and the customer later purchases, the PPC ad receives full credit for that conversion. This model is useful for understanding which channels are most effective at generating initial awareness. It is most effective for very short sales cycles and impulse buys.

2. **Last-Touch Attribution:** Contrary to first-touch, last-touch attribution gives all the credit to the final interaction before the conversion. If a customer sees several ads but clicks on an email link and then makes a purchase, the email campaign is considered wholly responsible for the sale. This model can be helpful in determining which marketing efforts are best at closing sales. This is the least accurate model because it neglects all the actions taken by the customer early on in the customer journey. When a customer is asked, "How did you find us?" the last touch is too often the answer.

3. **Multitouch Attribution:** Almost every purchase a customer makes requires multiple touches, therefore making this the holy grail. However, because many touches will be nondigital, purely visual, or simply forgotten, multitouch attribution models are more complex. They recognize that multiple interactions contribute to the final decision to purchase. There are various ways to implement multitouch attribution, such as:

- **Linear Model:** Each touchpoint in the customer journey is given equal credit for the sale.
- **Time-Decay Model:** Touchpoints closer in time to the sale receive more credit.
- **Position-Based Model:** This model might attribute more credit to the first and last touch, with remaining credit distributed among other touchpoints. This is often called a U-shaped model. Another similar model, called a W-shaped model, gives additional credit to touches in the middle of the journey.
- **Data-Driven Model:** This sophisticated approach uses algorithms to attribute credit to each touchpoint based on actual data and the observed impact on conversions. This model requires much more data and sophisticated analytics.

Multitouch attribution offers a nuanced view of the customer journey, acknowledging that different marketing tactics play various roles at different stages of the sales funnel. It can guide marketers on how to allocate budgets across the marketing mix for optimal results. However, it requires more advanced tracking and analysis capabilities.

To be clear, multitouch attribution is the model that would give the most accurate picture . . . if it was always possible. Because of its complexity, many organizations simply don't attempt it. The best approach is to establish which touches can be tracked, track as many as you can, and add those to your multitouch model with a clearly communicated understanding that every touch will not be tracked.

Multitouch attribution, while often heralded as the pinnacle of marketing attribution, is indeed a complex endeavor, revealing a panoramic view of the customer's journey through various marketing touchpoints. Its implementation can be a significant step toward aligning Sales and Marketing, as it paints a vivid picture of how each marketing action influences the customer leading up to a sale. This insight is invaluable in fostering a collaborative environment where both teams can see the contribution of marketing efforts to the sales pipeline.

However, the complexity of multitouch attribution models can sometimes be a double-edged sword, particularly regarding Sales and Marketing alignment. The granular data can be overwhelming and may lead to disagreements on which touchpoints truly drive conversions. The intricacy of data modeling and the allocation of credit among numerous interactions require a high degree of transparency and communication between Sales and Marketing to interpret the data correctly. This complexity necessitates a shared language and understanding as well as shared tools and platforms that can track and analyze customer interactions cohesively.

To benefit from multitouch attribution effectively, Sales and Marketing must work closely together to establish clear goals, understand the data's implications, and agree on how to act upon the insights gained. Regular meetings to discuss attribution reports can help ensure both teams are on the same page, facilitating a unified approach to refining strategies and tactics. By jointly analyzing the customer journey, both Sales and Marketing can identify and reinforce the most impactful touchpoints, leading to more efficient and targeted campaigns. This cooperative approach clarifies the role of Marketing in the sales process and also encourages a culture of shared responsibility and continuous improvement.

In the end, the goal of marketing attribution is to find out which marketing efforts lead to sales. The ideal approach, multitouch attribution, looks at all the ways customers interact with a business before buying something. Although in theory it would give the most complete picture, this model is complex and nearly impossible to thoroughly achieve; therefore fewer companies can use it.

Given all these measurement options, when Sales and Marketing teams work together to understand their data they can better see how their work leads to sales. They need to communicate well and analyze the customer's experience together to make the most effective marketing plans. By doing this, both teams can work better together, improve their strategies, and help the business grow.

Whom Does the Marketing Team Report To?

The entire ethos of a Marketing team can depend on whom the team reports to. And whom it reports to is often determined by the growth stage of the company.

At a pivotal juncture in my career, I reported to a CMO (chief marketing officer) whose expertise was actually in product development; in essence, he was a chief product officer with the title of CMO. He lacked experience in marketing, which became particularly ironic as the company was at a stage where scaling, driving revenue, and bolstering sales should have been the priority.

Aside from the need for a focus on these areas, the CMO leaned into the company's product roots, steering the Marketing team toward product-centric marketing. With the team being instructed to concentrate on product promotion and development, this misalignment was poorly timed and didn't align with the company's immediate needs, proving to be an ineffective strategy for the company's growth phase.

In the early stages of a company when the focus is intensely on product development and launch, Marketing teams might report to a product leader. This alignment makes sense in this context because the marketing efforts are primarily geared toward product launches and awareness. However, as the company grows and shifts its focus toward scaling and revenue generation, the structure often changes. Marketing might then report to a CRO (chief revenue officer) or a CMO, reflecting a greater alignment with sales processes and objectives. This shift is crucial for the Marketing team to move beyond product-centric activities to broader opportunity generation and sales support.

The evolution of the Marketing team's reporting structure should mirror the company's shifting priorities and strategies. When under a product leader, the Marketing team must tightly couple their efforts with the product life cycle, sometimes to the extent that their success and failure are intertwined with the product's performance.

On the other hand, when aligned with sales or revenue leaders, the focus should broaden beyond product promotion to also include lead generation, customer acquisition, and direct support of the sales process. This realignment is essential for Marketing teams to contribute more effectively to the company's overall revenue goals and to move out of being seen purely as a cost center.

Imagine a software or technology company in its inception phase, with a focus on developing a unique software solution. Initially, the Marketing team should be under the leadership of a product division head because the company's priority is to ensure the product fits the market need. The Marketing team's efforts are heavily invested in promoting the features of the software, driving beta user sign-ups, and collecting user feedback to inform product development. Their success is measured by user acquisition rates and the relevance of user feedback, which is critical for product iteration.

As the company's product gains traction and the focus shifts toward growth and profitability, the Marketing team doesn't abruptly change management but should gradually transition to report to a revenue-focused leader (such as a chief revenue officer). This transition might occur through a series of strategic planning sessions, alignment meetings, and restructuring efforts to ensure that the Marketing team's new KPIs align with sales targets. The marketing initiatives are now geared toward lead generation, nurturing leads into sales-ready prospects and supporting the Sales team with materials to close deals. The Marketing team's contribution is now directly linked to sales performance metrics like lead conversion rates and sales revenue.

But what if the alignment of the Marketing team's leadership does not match the company's current objectives? Of the many unfortunate scenarios that could play out, here are a couple.

Let's say a company is in its early start-up stage, where the primary focus should be on refining the product and achieving product-market fit. Instead, the Marketing team reports to a chief revenue officer whose objectives are centered on revenue growth and sales. In this setup, the Marketing team is driven to prioritize lead generation and conversion tactics over building product awareness and engagement. This premature push for revenue can lead to a situation where marketing campaigns are more aggressive in sales promotion without adequately considering whether the product meets the nuanced needs of the targeted customers.

The result is a potential misalignment where the product may not yet be ready for the scale at which it's being marketed, leading to customer dissatisfaction and increased churn rates and potentially harming the company's long-term reputation.

Conversely, let's consider a company at a stage where the initial product-market fit has been established and the need of the hour is to scale and increase revenue. However, the Marketing team continues to report to the product leadership, which is more focused on product features and development rather than market expansion and customer acquisition strategies. As a result, the Marketing team is preoccupied with product-centric campaigns, emphasizing features and updates rather than creating targeted messaging to attract new market segments or reinforce the value proposition to potential large-scale customers.

The mismatch in leadership focus could mean that Marketing's efforts do not fully support the Sales team in lead generation, resulting in missed opportunities for growth and lower-than-expected revenue figures. This misalignment can lead to a competitive disadvantage, as the company is not capitalizing on its established market presence to scale effectively.

Understanding this dynamic is vital for any business looking to optimize its marketing efforts in line with its growth stage and overarching business objectives. In both scenarios, the misalignment of the Marketing team's reporting structure with the company's stage of growth underscores the importance of having the right leadership focus on ensuring marketing efforts are synchronized with the company's strategic goals. This synchronization is crucial for effectively leveraging marketing resources and maximizing the impact on the company's growth trajectory.

Now, what if you're on a Marketing team where neither leadership nor reporting structure is going to change? What if you regularly introduce new products even though your company and reporting hierarchy are well established? My advice is that smaller Marketing teams must be agile and adaptable to effectively support both product development phases and revenue generation phases. Having clarity of these phases in mind and communicating with all involved—leadership, Sales, and Marketing—can make for an open conversation about priorities and marketing focus.

In larger, more mature companies, these phases will constantly overlap. And as we'll discuss later, there must be marketers who are positioned and skilled for both areas of focus. As businesses and their teams grow, there should be a consideration of establishing permanent teams for each area of growth. This means teams or people whose primary and consistent focus is on one of the areas—product marketing, demand generation, or brand growth.

Expert Insight—Matt Crisp

Matt Crisp is an entrepreneur and private investor. He is the cofounder and former principal at eVestment Alliance LLC, a company that provides institutional investment data and analytics. As the chief operating officer (COO) of eVestment, Crisp played a key role in establishing and growing the company, which was eventually acquired by NASDAQ in 2017.

Matt shares his insights on corporate hierarchies and how misalignment between Sales and Marketing gave rise to the role of the CRO—chief revenue officer:

> I didn't really start hearing the term "chief revenue officer" until maybe 2016 or 2017. We were starting to see SaaS companies hire a chief revenue officer. And we started asking the question, "What's the difference between that and the global head of sales?"

> Our private equity investors said, "Well, you get misalignment between Sales and Marketing. This person sits on top of both and understands both." And it made a lot of sense. Now you see companies where that role has really evolved and become a big-time role for a lot of high-growth companies.

> It did give CMOs who understood Sales the opportunity to move up in the executive stack even further. Again, for years, once you'd become the chief marketing officer, that was probably as high as you were going to get in corporate. Because on the Sales side, the global head of sales could make his or her way to becoming the CEO. There are a lot of CEOs with a Sales background. You didn't see that as much from the Marketing side, but now the CRO gave CMOs the ability (if they understood Sales—exactly to your point in this book) to move up in the executive stack one level. It just

gave a little more upward mobility for some of the people on
the Marketing side.

Navigating Whom Marketing Reports To

Whom Marketing reports to matters greatly in how Marketing is both perceived and measured. Whether directly reporting to the chief marketing officer (CMO), chief production officer (CPO), chief revenue officer (CRO), or other leadership, it is important to understand how to correctly support that leadership.

Here's how you can navigate this dual mandate with your Marketing team:

Develop a Dual Marketing Team Mindset

Developing a dual mindset within a Marketing team calls for a blend of flexibility and strategic focus. Marketers must embrace the dual objectives of nurturing the product's market fit while also fueling the sales pipeline. This requires an understanding that their role is not static; it evolves with each product life cycle and sales quarter. To achieve this, they must internalize the customer's perspective, exploring not just how a product fits into the market but also how it resolves specific pain points, which, in turn, informs compelling narratives for sales enablement.

Simultaneously, they must pivot toward thinking like sales strategists, analyzing market data, anticipating customer needs, and crafting messages that resonate at different stages of the buyer's journey. This dual mindset means that every marketing initiative is evaluated through a bifocal lens: How does it serve the product's positioning and the company's revenue goals?

By harmonizing these two perspectives, marketers can create campaigns that are both informative and impactful, driving product adoption and sales concurrently. It's a dynamic way of operating that places equal importance on long-term brand building and immediate sales support, ensuring that the Marketing team remains an integral contributor to both product success and the company's financial health.

Leverage Cross-Functional Collaboration

Leveraging cross-functional collaboration is pivotal for a Marketing team working under a fixed leadership structure while regularly introducing new products. It involves breaking down silos and fostering a culture of communication and cooperation across the organization. Marketing professionals must proactively reach out to and engage with colleagues in product development, sales, customer service, and other relevant departments to ensure a cohesive approach to product support and revenue generation.

This collaboration begins with understanding the different languages spoken across departments—from the technical lingo of the Product team to the customer-centric dialect of Sales—and translating them into a unified marketing message that resonates with both internal stakeholders and the target audience. Regularly scheduled meetings with cross-functional teams provide opportunities for the Marketing team to glean insights from product developers about upcoming features or from Sales about customer pain points and objections encountered in the field.

Leveraging collaboration tools can play a crucial role in fostering this synergy. Shared platforms where teams can update each other in real time about changes in customer sentiment, market conditions, or product development timelines help ensure that marketing strategies remain agile and informed. We'll get into this more in the Systems part of the book.

By cementing these collaborative relationships, Marketing can ensure that their strategies and campaigns are consistently aligned with the company's broader objectives. They can provide the Sales team with the tools and insights needed to close deals while also ensuring that product messaging remains accurate and compelling. Such cross-functional collaboration doesn't just benefit the Marketing team—it creates a more unified, efficient, and responsive organization where every department contributes to the company's success with a shared understanding and purpose.

Customize Metrics and Key Performance Indicators

Customizing metrics and KPIs is essential for Marketing teams to effectively support product growth and drive revenue. The essence of this customization is to capture a wide array of data points that reflect the multifaceted role of Marketing. For instance, while product growth can be tracked through user engagement metrics, feature adoption rates, and customer satisfaction scores, revenue generation might be measured by leads, conversion rates, average deal size, and sales cycle lengths. The Marketing team must choose these metrics wisely and also seek to understand the story behind the numbers, interpreting what they indicate about customer behavior and market trends.

This data-driven approach enables marketers to adjust their strategies in real time, tailoring their efforts to what the numbers reveal. They must set clear, measurable goals that align with both product milestones and sales targets, ensuring that every campaign is purpose-driven and results-oriented. By customizing these metrics, they can identify which initiatives drive product adoption, which bolster the sales pipeline, and where there are opportunities for optimization.

Ultimately, by selecting the right metrics and KPIs, Marketing can demonstrate their dual contribution to the organization. They can show how their work raises product awareness and drives user acquisition as well as how it directly impacts the bottom line. This balance is crucial for justifying marketing spend and for highlighting the department's role as both a guardian of the product's reputation and a catalyst for the company's revenue growth.

Segment the Marketing Team into Units

In larger organizations where this is feasible, segmenting the Marketing team into specialized units is a proactive approach to ensure that each facet of the company's objectives is given dedicated attention and expertise. This strategy involves structuring the Marketing department into at least two units, each with a focus on distinct aspects of the overall marketing strategy. One segment could concentrate on the intricacies of product marketing—understanding product features, developing messaging that resonates with the target audience, and creating materials that highlight the product's unique selling points. Another segment would focus on the broader picture of driving demand—crafting campaigns that generate leads, nurturing those leads through the sales funnel, and providing the Sales team with the tools and insights they need to close deals.

By segmenting the Marketing team, the company ensures that while one group is fine-tuning the product narrative and aligning it with customer needs, another is aggressively identifying and capturing market opportunities that contribute to the sales pipeline. This division allows for a depth of focus that a single, undivided team might struggle to achieve, ensuring that both the product and revenue goals are pursued with equal intensity and expertise.

Furthermore, each team member can become a specialist in a specific area, improving campaign effectiveness and fostering a sense of ownership and accountability for the role they play in the company's success. This segmentation, when managed well, facilitates a more agile and responsive marketing operation that can simultaneously champion the product and drive the company's growth.

Incorporate Continuous Cross-Functional Education

Incorporating continuous cross-functional education, particularly with the inclusion of Sales team members and leaders, is vital for a Marketing team tasked with balancing product and revenue objectives. This approach to learning bridges the gap between different departments, enhancing the team's ability to understand and contribute to varied aspects of the business. Continuous education in this context involves regular training sessions that cover the latest trends and techniques in marketing and should also include the fundamentals of sales strategies, product development processes, and customer service excellence.

By understanding the principles and challenges of other functions, marketers gain a more holistic view of the business, enabling them to craft messages and strategies that resonate across all departments. This cross-functional knowledge is particularly important in a dynamic business environment where the lines between product management, Sales, and Marketing are increasingly blurred. This lends to the importance of shared experiences or "shadowing" days that can provide practical, hands-on experience across teams.

Revenue team education can take many forms, from in-house workshops led by different department heads to external seminars and online courses that cover a broad spectrum of topics. For example, the framework outlined in this book is available as a full-day CASH workshop that can be given as a sales kick-off event. These types of training should include both Sales and Marketing teams. Encouraging participation in cross-departmental projects and training can do more than educate your teams; it can help them understand and respect each other better.

Create Agile Marketing Campaigns

Creating agile campaigns means building marketing strategies that are effective as well as flexible enough to adapt to changing market conditions, product developments, and sales needs. For a Marketing team that supports both product and revenue objectives, agility in campaign planning and execution is even more important. This includes developing campaigns that can quickly pivot or be modified based on real-time data, feedback from Sales teams, or shifts in the product road map.

Agile campaigns start with a deep understanding of the target audience and clear, measurable goals, but are also designed with the flexibility to evolve. This might involve creating a range of content and marketing materials that can be quickly customized for different contexts or audiences. For instance, a core set of digital assets can be repurposed with slight modifications to support a new product feature announcement, a special sales initiative, or a response to a competitor's move.

Agile campaigns can also be data-driven. They rely heavily on analytics and feedback loops to assess performance and make adjustments in real time. This approach allows the Marketing team to test different messages, channels, and tactics, learning what works best and adapting strategy accordingly. Regular communication with the Sales team and other departments ensures that marketing efforts are aligned with the latest business developments and priorities.

Investing in marketing automation tools can also facilitate agility. These tools can help segment audiences, personalize messages, schedule communications, and track results, making it easier to manage and adjust campaigns efficiently.

In essence, creating agile campaigns means being prepared to iterate and evolve strategies quickly. It means having a plan while also being ready to change that plan based on new insights, market trends, or internal company changes. This approach ensures that marketing efforts remain relevant, effective, and aligned with the company's immediate and long-term objectives.

By taking these steps, the Marketing team can become a versatile unit capable of supporting the company's objectives regardless of the static nature of the reporting hierarchy. The key is to maintain a strategic perspective that aligns marketing activities with both product and revenue priorities, ensuring the team is contributing effectively to the company's overall success.

Expert Insight—Sandy Carter

Sandy Carter is a distinguished technology executive with an impressive career spanning multiple Fortune 100 companies, including Amazon Web Services, IBM, and Unstoppable Domains, where she has held diverse C-level positions such as chief operations officer, chief marketing officer, chief product officer, and chief revenue officer. A pioneer in AI innovation, Carter played a crucial role in the development of IBM's Watson and introduced groundbreaking business models for the AI ecosystem, shaping AI tooling and the application of advanced language models.

Sandy shares her thoughts on leadership, the CRO, and shared metrics:

One of the best things companies can do is have that strong collaboration between Sales and Marketing. For me, making sure that you have empathetic leaders is really the start of that. If you look at my background and my history, I have been a chief sales officer and I've been a chief marketing officer. And so now when I go into either one of those roles or even a CRO role, like I am in today, it enables me to see both sides. Because both sides have to be able to be empathetic to the other's challenges in order to effectively work together. I know a lot of organizations feel that they're going to almost coin-operate marketing. You know; put in a quarter and out come two dollars. But marketing is not coin-operated, so I think it's really important for the Sales team to recognize that there is a process and there are mechanisms for marketing, but marketing is also creative and intuitive.

Sometimes there are going to be failures that you have to pivot around and then really drive better results. And on the Sales side, I think marketers need to realize that it's not one and done either. When they create a lead, a seller doesn't just grab the lead and immediately go close them. There's a lot of work that has to go in around it, a lot of art. I would also say that goes into crafting the deal specifically for that particular customer as well. For example, this morning I'm the CRO and we are working on closing a deal. And part of what the deal requires is strong co-marketing with the customer.

So, we brought in both parties, and of course, Sales is like, "Just tell them what they want to hear so I can close the deal." And the Marketing team is like, "No. I want to make sure that if we agree on a co-marketing plan, it's going to work." The worst thing would be to close the deal and just agree with them and then not have the results come out. So, I jumped in and gave good points to Marketing and good points to Sales, and they came up with a killer plan that closed the deal. I think that's really one of the best things that you can do, is to have that collaboration.

The second piece is to have a shared metric system. I really hate it when you've got one set of metrics for your sellers and a different set for your marketeers. For example, a lot of times, your Marketing team will be measured only on awareness. Well, for a Sales team, that's good, but that's just the start of the customer funnel. You need to make sure that at least somebody on the Marketing team has responsibility for the brand and for awareness, but someone's also measured on lead creation and the quality of those leads as you're marching through that customer funnel. I think that would be the two tops—that your teams are empathetic to each other, understanding where each one comes from, and that you have a similar metric structure.

Chapter 8

Lee's Ps of Marketing

The concept of the Four Ps of marketing, also known as the marketing mix, originated with Neil Borden who introduced the idea in the 1940s. Borden's initial concept encompassed a multitude of factors that influenced marketing outcomes. His student, E. Jerome McCarthy, later refined these into the more streamlined framework known today as the Four Ps: product, price, place, and promotion.

These concepts have not stood the test of time very well. They reflect a time before Sales and Marketing were required to understand each other's roles and when Marketing was allowed to work in a silo away from business results.

I contend that if modern marketers work within the boundaries of that dated framework, their careers will be short or the business they work for will struggle.

Here is an updated and more effective framework:

* * *

Lee's Ps

Presence

Perception

Price

Profitability

* * *

I'll explain the three items I've dropped from the list in a moment. First, here are Lee's Ps:

Presence

Having a desired product or service is not enough. It must be present in conversations, social feeds, and communities in order for desire for the product to grow. Many great products have failed simply because content about them wasn't present in consumers' minds enough to foster sales growth. At the same time, countless numbers of products have grown in demand and sales long before the product or service even existed. This is proof that the mental and social presence of a product is more important than its actual existence. Presence can grow a brand or product on its own, regardless of promotional tactics. Just ask Ocean Spray. In 2020, after Nathan Apodaca uploaded a video of himself skateboarding and drinking an Ocean Spray cranberry juice from the bottle, the brand went viral, and sales increased. All of this was without an Ocean Spray-initiated promotion tactic.

Perception

Because of the ability to have instant global conversations, perception of a product can instantly rocket a product into viral success or immediately cancel the product and make it shameful to consume. Whether it's the toxic product that is perceived to be helpful in saving the environment or the cheaply made handbag that gives the consumer a feeling of being rich, perception rules buyer behavior, and this is why I consider it a primary P in this marketing mix.

Price

Price is often the first checkpoint in the customer journey. If customers perceive that they cannot obtain an item solely based on price shock, they may move away even before considering a potential purchase.

Price is the linchpin between perception and profitability.

A prospect that perceives a value equal to or greater than your price will likely accept that price and desire to be a customer. If that price also provides a profitability margin for your business, that makes the prospect desirable to you as a customer. The price must serve both the customer and your business for it to be effective.

Profitability

Even if you set a price to fit a market, can that market sustain your business at that price point? After all, you can't get blood from a turnip.

No matter the price of your product, the customers you target must be able to consistently provide you with a profit at a price you set for them. If it is too costly to service a market, then your profit margins shrink and serving that market no longer makes sense. Lowering the price doesn't work for you and raising it doesn't work for the customers.

With the ideal target audience, profitability is only limited by how well you market the product. As long as the market can afford it and you clearly market the product to fit people's perception of value and need, you can price your product in a way that fits your desired profit.

* * *

Here are the three items I removed from the traditional list and why:

Promotion: I use the term "presence" rather than "promotion" because promotion referred to a tactic taken solely by Marketing. It also implies that it is fully the Marketing team's effort to convince the customer to make a purchase. What has changed is that social media allows a product to take on a promotional life of its own in the form of viral presence. As mentioned in my description of presence, once an item establishes its place in the minds of the consumer, the promotion takes on a life of its own. Sure, promotion tactics may spark presence, but promotion alone does not drive the success of a business at a time when word of mouth and social influence can make or break the success of a product.

Product: Effective marketing can happen even before a product exists; therefore, I believe that having the product as a part of the marketing mix is obsolete. While having a good product does make marketing easier, products don't exist to serve marketing's need. Marketing exists to serve products. In our fast-paced digital reality, marketing is a part of the product mix—not the opposite.

Place: While place may be a factor in consuming your product or service, it does not need to be a factor in the marketing of it. Outside of personal services or environmentally based businesses, place is becoming more obsolete each day in a globally connected world. Marketing targets people, not the spaces where they spend time or consume products. You don't have to be in a particular place to learn about a product. Algorithms will place products in front of you no matter where you are—digitally or physically. You can be targeted with content no matter what media or social channels you use. If you want something, it can conveniently come to you; locational logistics is no longer a significant factor.

Profit-Centric Marketing

If you've ever seen me speak on stage or attended one of my workshops, you'd quickly notice my candid style, especially when addressing the pressing issues in Sales and Marketing in the current business climate. At a particular B2B marketing conference, I directly told marketers, "If you are in this room right now, you are among those most likely to retain your job next year." This remark was rooted in a critical topic from this book—the necessity for marketers to assimilate the revenue-centric vernacular of sales into their strategies.

You may also recall my earlier story about the box of plastic pork chops that a previous Marketing team left me. It was the epitome of what it looks like when the Marketing team wants to be seen as a cost center. That team (which no longer existed) was viewed by the Sales team as the group that made T-shirts, planned trade shows, and bought tchotchkes (cheap trinkets) to give away. All that was left of that team when I was hired was a box of plastic pork chops. All cost center.

To shift from a cost to a profit center, marketers must deepen their engagement with the sales cycle, using metrics that resonate with sales outcomes. By focusing on the financial impact of their campaigns, such as how marketing initiatives shorten the sales cycle or improve lead quality, they can demonstrate their contributions to the company's bottom line. Metrics should be chosen for their direct link to sales results, including customer acquisition cost and lifetime value.

Marketers' regular dialogue with the Sales team garners insights into the field's realities, informing more potent and sales-aligned marketing strategies. Such collaboration ensures Marketing's role in creating per-suasive content that accelerates the buyer's journey toward a purchase.

To solidify Marketing's strategic position, professionals must consistently articulate the quantitative impact of their work. Data-driven reports that correlate marketing actions with sales metrics like lead conversion and revenue growth will showcase Marketing's direct support of the Sales team and broader company goals.

By embedding marketing activities within the sales narrative and cali-brating strategies to amplify the sales process, Marketing enhances their strategic value. This realignment advocates for Marketing's indispensable role as well as serves to underscore their contribution to business growth, thereby securing a position as a fundamental asset to the company's financial health and success.

Part 3

C
A
Systems
H

Systems form the backbone of any organization. They encapsulate essential processes and the tools necessary for execution. At the heart of these systems are the people who contribute to them, operate them, and carefully select the tools that best support their businesses. Part 3 will explore how technology, people, and the design of Sales and Marketing interactions play a central role in the effectiveness of these teams working efficiently to drive revenue.

Chapter 9

Marketing and Sales Systems

What Are Your "Systems"?

On the same day I started drafting this chapter, I sent a reminder to our Sales team to shift inactive opportunities to the "nurture" track in our CRM. To some, this might seem like a trivial administrative chore. Yet this simple step is part of a larger, effective system that has repeatedly driven new sales. In our setup, moving a deal to "nurture" triggers a series of customized emails designed to keep our brand in the client's mind.

It's a strategy that has paid off handsomely. For instance, one of our largest deals this year was secured not for the initial product of interest, but for an alternative offering highlighted in our follow-up emails. Wins like this hinge on two things: belief in the efficacy of our systems and consistent execution of each task within these systems.

Reflecting on security technologist Bruce Schneier's concept of people, process, and technology, we see a similar pattern. However, in our definition of "systems," there's a distinct emphasis on the synergy between these elements. It's this combination of the right processes, the appropriate tools, and the people who bring them together that defines a system in its entirety. Each component is pivotal: Processes outline the steps to be taken, tools provide the means for execution, and people make the strategic decisions and actions that drive the system forward.

People

Before you get to tools, the center of your system is your people. Your salespeople and marketers run the revenue system. If you were building out a team of salespeople and marketers, whom would you want on that team?

Of course, you want the best salespeople and the best marketers available, but to build out a unified team that truly works as a system to build revenue, you'll need to find people who have (or can be trained to have) a true understanding and respect for the other teammates' skill sets.

Imagine a spectrum where, on the far left, you've got your marketer who is not successful in contributing to closed deals. And on the far right, there's the salesperson with no market to sell to. You don't want either of these extremes; they're bad for business and customer relationships. The perfect combination of Sales and Marketing is dead center—we'll call the team members in that spot the unicorn. Halfway to the left of the unicorn, as shown in Figure 8.1, you'll spot the ideal marketer, and halfway to the right, there's the ideal salesperson.

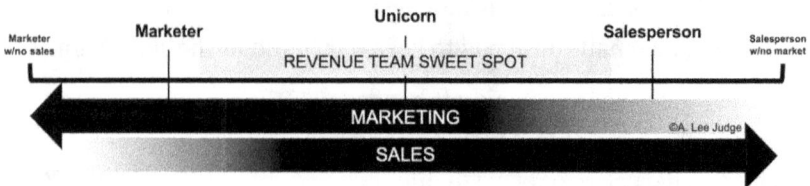

Figure 8.1 The Revenue Team Sweet Spot

To examine a more realistic goal, let's focus on the gold mine here: the wider center area we'll call the "Revenue Team Sweet Spot." This is the zone that stretches from just over halfway to the ideal marketer all the way to over halfway to the ideal salesperson. Why is this the sweet spot?

Simple. If you have team members who land here, you have marketers who understand the essentials of Sales and salespeople who get the nuances of Marketing. These are versatile professionals who can harmonize sales and marketing strategies in a way that maximizes revenue and enhances customer relationships.

So when you're building your Revenue team, aim to recruit or develop talent that lands in this sweet spot. They bring the best of both worlds to the table, making them invaluable assets for driving business growth.

Tools

Now that we have our people selected, let's look at our tools. This selection is a deliberate act aimed at supporting your people and enhancing the overall effectiveness of the revenue processes. Sales and Marketing teams rely on a suite of tools to streamline their processes and enhance productivity:

Customer Relationship Management (CRM): CRM systems, which are foundational for tracking customer interactions, oversee sales pipelines and store valuable customer data. This information is the core of what is needed for Sales professionals to personalize their follow-ups and build strong customer relationships.

Marketing Automation Platforms (MAPs): MAPs complement CRMs by automating the delivery of marketing campaigns and nurturing leads with scheduled outreach. These platforms can also score leads, helping prioritize follow-up based on a prospect's engagement level. Analytics tools are another piece of the puzzle, offering deep dives into customer behavior and campaign effectiveness, allowing for data-driven strategy adjustments.

Content Management Systems (CMSs): CMSs enable the swift update and management of website content, ensuring the material remains current and engaging. For social media initiatives, content management tools are indispensable. They schedule content, engage with users, and analyze traffic and engagement data.

Email Marketing Tools: Email marketing tools are specialized for designing mass email campaigns, managing lists of subscribers, and tracking engagement metrics. These tools often integrate with CRMs for enhanced personalization and audience segmentation.

Prospecting Tools: Prospecting tools are invaluable assets for Sales teams, designed to help identify, research, and engage potential customers efficiently. These tools provide useful insights and data about prospects, including contact information, company details, and behavior patterns. For instance, platforms like LinkedIn Sales Navigator allow Sales professionals to tap into a vast network to find and connect with key decision-makers. Tools such as ZoomInfo offer extensive databases of business information, helping Sales teams target their outreach precisely. Meanwhile, tools like Outreach automate and manage interactions, ensuring that follow-ups are timely and organized. By leveraging these prospecting tools, Sales teams can streamline lead generation, focus on high-potential prospects, and enhance their overall efficiency in the sales process.

While some of these tools may be perceived as tools for the Marketing team, they all work together to enable Sales to do a better and more productive job. Often these tools are bundled together and labeled as a "platform." These platforms or individual tools work together to provide Sales teams with easy access to resources, tailored content for different buyer stages, and insights into which materials help close deals.

Again, these tools should not function in isolation. When they're part of a well-oiled system, they form a comprehensive ecosystem that allows for seamless data exchange, offering a holistic view of the customer journey. For example, a CRM can segment audiences for targeted campaigns in the MAP, which can then be fine-tuned using insights from the email marketing tool. Meanwhile, the CMS ensures that all content is consistent, current, and available, while the social media tools amplify the reach. This interconnectivity empowers businesses to make strategic, data-informed decisions that resonate with their objectives and customer needs.

A robust system, empowered by the right tools, can elevate an organization's efficiency, accuracy, and productivity. The tools we choose should seamlessly integrate into our processes, enhancing them without causing disruptions. They should offer solutions that simplify tasks, automate repetitive work, and provide insightful data that leads to better decision-making.

While it's the processes that should ideally shape the selection of tools, it's also the responsibility of the team to understand and harness these tools to their full potential.

Aligning Tools within Processes

Let's examine the relationship between processes and tools in greater depth and discuss why most practitioners advise that you have your processes dictate the tools you adopt—with an exception I'll explain.

Generally, it's advisable to let the process dictate the choice of tool, not the other way around. However, there are exceptions. Sometimes a business may be so deeply invested in a particular tool that switching to a different one for the sole reason of adhering to this guideline becomes impractical.

A common issue I've observed is executives, often with limited understanding of day-to-day operations, rigidly adhering to the "process-first" approach. For the sake of being process-first, they regularly cause the addition of new tools for each new process because the established tool doesn't bend to the new process. This can lead to an unnecessary accumulation of tools in the marketing and sales technology stack. To make things worse, they might retain an established tool that's no longer efficient simply because it's too deeply integrated, too deeply invested, or costs the organization too much to get out of.

You most often see this with enterprise-level CRMs. The bigger and more customizable the CRM, the harder and costlier it is to get out of. This inevitably results in the request for new tools to fit new processes, which then leads to technology bloat—an excessive number of tools creating a counterproductive cycle.

The big takeaway? Businesses should strive to align their technology with their strategic goals and operational needs. This means not confining processes to the limitations of existing technology while also being mindful not to add new tools for every single new process. The goal is to create a balanced, efficient tech environment that supports your business's overall strategy and operational efficiency.

Selecting Technology to Fit Your System

Before we look at how Sales and Marketing teams can use their software systems to bring cohesiveness, let's back up to the moment when an organization selects software for their teams to use.

This is where I urge you to avoid the TV/VCR dilemma.

You see, once upon a time—long, long ago—people watched their recorded media on large cassette tapes they played in a device called a VCR (video cassette recorder). At some point, television manufacturers thought it would be convenient to create a combined electronic device that married the TV and the VCR into one—a TV/VCR. The only problem was that the TVs far outlasted the VCRs. Even the TV *technology* outlasted the VCR. That left people stuck with TVs that had this unusable, outdated device welded to the bottom of their otherwise useful television. Buying the combo device was not a good purchase decision in the long run. Buying a TV and a separate VCR would have felt like the better choice when the new digital video discs (DVDs) were introduced. Remember this scenario when choosing software for your sales and marketing functions.

When selecting software for your organization, it's crucial to remember one fundamental rule: Prioritize purpose, performance, and longevity over all-in-one convenience. This is not unlike hiring for your team—you wouldn't opt for a jack-of-all-trades who performs moderately in several areas over a specialist who excels in one critical role. Similarly, when you invest in software, ensure it is the best in its class for the tasks it's intended to perform—and lasts long enough to give ROI.

That's not to say there's no room for multifunction software solutions. An all-in-one platform that combines a customer relationship management system, email marketing tools, automation capabilities, and other sales and marketing functions can indeed be a powerful asset. Yet it's important to note that few platforms can genuinely claim to excel across multiple functions. As someone who has been the administrator of many such business tools, I can assure you that each of them will have weak points that reveal how they tacked on an additional underdeveloped feature in order to sell their core competency.

The key is to identify your priority needs and discern what requires best-of-class software versus what can function adequately as an add-on. For instance, if you're primarily in need of a CRM system and don't have a dedicated Marketing team, a top-tier CRM platform with added marketing features may be sufficient, even if those additional features are not best in class.

On the other hand, if your Marketing team is spearheading the software selection and requires advanced marketing automation capabilities, you might not want to replace your existing CRM with a combo software just because it offers high-end marketing features but has a subpar CRM component. In such a scenario, you'd be better served by best-in-class marketing software that has strong integration capabilities with your existing CRM.

In a nutshell, the aim should always be to choose the best software combination for your organization without compromising the overall effectiveness due to any single component's inadequacy. Your goal is not just to check all the boxes but to ensure each box is checked with the highest standard of functionality and performance.

Here's a sidenote from my days purchasing enterprise software: Before purchasing a software tool, work your way past the software salespeople and get to the engineers who work on the software. They will be more honest about what the platform can and cannot do. They will be both proud of their work and critical of it. They will also give hints about what the software was initially built to do versus what it is being sold as. Software salespeople will push the envelope and sell where the software hopes to be in the future. The engineers are more likely to tell you exactly how developed the software is *today*. However, it's important to understand that a software Sales team does not want you talking to the developers, so plan your prepurchase detective work smartly.

System Ownership

I was on my very first business trip with some colleagues. The oldest of us was 25 years old at best and he was driving us to the meeting. In the middle of our drive, at about 55 miles per hour, he suddenly pulls the emergency break of the car. "Why did you do that?" I yelled. "You're going to ruin the break!"

His response was . . . "It's a rental—what do I care?" That stuck in my head as an example of some people's attitude regarding the way they treat things they do not own.

Today, when on stage talking to Sales and Marketing leaders about their business processes, I ask them this question: "Have you ever washed a rental car?" I almost never get a hand raise.

It's because people tend to take less care of things that they do not own. If Marketing has no ownership in the CRM and Sales has no ownership in the marketing automation platform, neither will assist in taking care of the system perceived to be owned by the other.

As a Sales and Marketing Operations practitioner, it was often my job to get members of Sales and Marketing to work in each other's software platforms. This usually came with a level of reluctance because, as members of one team or the other, there was an attitude of "that" software was for "them," not "us." Still today, this perception is not made any easier by the company and product names of the software that we use.

Popular brands in sales use the word "sales" in their brand names—Salesforce, for example. And the products targeted toward salespeople use terms attractive to sales software buyers—like "sales hub," "sales engage," and "sales cloud."

Likewise, you would find marketing terms like "campaign," "contact," and "marketing cloud" in the names of products and brands targeted toward marketing software buyers.

Fortunately, software platforms continue to become more cohesive due to the awareness that sales and marketing functions are intertwined. Being aware of this, these platform providers are doing better at giving their products more neutral names. However, this doesn't mean that there are not still challenges in getting the people and processes aligned.

Each team must be shown the value of the information in the systems they are reluctant to use. They must be given the understanding of how data flows from one system to another, where their data originates, and how they can use the data to perform their job better. That last part is the most crucial—*how they can perform their job better.* Even if they don't own the system, they still care about how it can benefit them. Showing them the WIIFM (the What's in It For Me?) is the key to making one team care about another team's platform.

Chapter 10

The System's Role in Alignment

As a reminder, the system isn't defined solely as the software tools. It also consists of the people who contribute to them and how they work together. Just as the Sales and Marketing teams must avoid working in a silo, in order for the CASH framework to operate the components of the framework are also interdependent. For *alignment* to work, the *system* must work. And for the *system* to work, there must be co-ownership of the tools, the inputs, and the reported outcomes from the system.

Here are actions you must take to encourage cohesive ownership of the Sales and Marketing systems.

Collaborative System Customization

Encouraging both Sales and Marketing to actively participate in the development of CRM and marketing systems can create a sense of shared ownership. This involvement can range from input on customized features and workflows to decision-making on software updates.

When both teams contribute to the system's evolution, a sense of shared ownership naturally emerges. Involving one team in the development of what is perceived as the other team's software fosters a shared sense of responsibility and collaboration.

For example, allow your Marketing team to assist in the development of the CRM. This will allow them to align data points (fields) across platforms, create reports showing Marketing's impact, and ensure that Sales gets a view of the customer data needed to help communicate with customers. This technical connection is the root of sales enablement—at the software level of the system. Organizations that realize the value of a Marketing Operations role benefit greatly here.

On the flip side, involve Sales in the setup and integration of the marketing automation platform into the CRM. This will ensure that Marketing is getting timely information regarding Sales activity, customer journeys, and successful deal closings. In order for Marketing to help push prospects toward a closed deal, it must have access to touchpoints and objections that Sales encounters. This helps Marketing to counter with actions to assist in pushing the deal along. Also, this connection allows automation within Marketing's software to react to the needs of both the Sales team and customers.

Cross-Team System Training Initiatives

To create a truly synergistic environment between Sales and Marketing, implementing regular cross-team training sessions is crucial. These sessions serve multiple purposes. First, they demystify the tools and systems used by each team. When a salesperson understands the mechanics of the marketing automation platform, or when a marketer gets to grips with the intricacies of the CRM system, something powerful happens. The tools no longer seem like foreign entities used only by the other team; they become familiar, less intimidating, and something they can also take ownership of.

The benefits of cross-training can extend far beyond familiarity. When team members grasp how their actions within one system influence outcomes in another, they begin to see the bigger picture. They can see how a well-qualified lead from Marketing funneled through the CRM can streamline the Sales process, or how feedback from Sales can help Marketing hone their campaigns for better targeting and lead generation. It encourages a more thoughtful and responsible approach to how each team uses their respective systems.

This kind of training fosters a sense of shared ownership. It breaks down the "us-versus-them" mindset and builds a united front where everyone is working toward the same business objectives. It's not about Marketing or Sales going it alone; it's about how both departments can contribute to the customer's journey and the company's bottom line.

Beyond sessions focused on the "tools" part of the system, this training should also involve scenario-based learning. Teams can run through exercises that simulate a lead moving from initial marketing conversion all the way through to sales conversion and close. These scenarios help cement an understanding of each other's roles and challenges.

Regular refresher courses and updates on system enhancements keep both teams on the cutting edge of functionality. As new features are added or processes updated, cross-team training ensures that no one is left behind and that the entire Revenue team is moving forward in lockstep.

By committing to these initiatives, a company fosters a culture of continuous learning and collaboration. This is an investment in skills as well as an investment in creating a cohesive, high-performing team that understands and values the contributions of each of its members.

Finally, integrated training sessions for both CRM and MAP systems can serve to educate and also build empathy between teams. When each team understands the challenges and capabilities of the tools their colleagues use, respect grows and a genuine partnership is formed.

Expert Insight—Darrell Alfonso

Darrell Alfonso is a prominent figure in the fields of marketing technology (Martech) and Marketing Operations (MOps). He has held such roles as the director of marketing strategy and operations at Indeed.com and has over 15 years of experience managing marketing technology for start-ups and leading enterprises, including Amazon Web Services.

Darrell shares his thoughts on the importance of collaboration at the systems level for Sales and Marketing:

I see it all the time. People say, "I don't want to learn about what that other team is doing," or "I don't care," or "How does their work affect mine? I just need to do my job." That silo-ish mentality needs to be broken down. And I think that also starts with the leaders too. And it's also an ego thing. If you think understanding customer data is not going to make you better as a salesperson in what you're going to say and how your outreach is going to be, you're completely wrong. That's the reality of what's happening. And vice versa.

If marketers don't know what customers are saying to salespeople as objections, how can they write that in their copy? How can they fix customer problems that they don't even know about? So, I think you need to drop your ego and say, "To be a good marketer, to be a good salesperson, I need to know about the customer data. I need to know about the sales activities. I need to know about what's going on across the aisle because it's what makes what I'm doing stronger."

Creating Cohesive Performance Metrics

It's essential to develop key performance indicators (KPIs) that necessitate contributions from both CRM and MAP, reflecting a consistent alignment across all platforms. For example, a KPI centered on lead conversion rates can prompt the Marketing team to supply superior leads via the MAP, whereas the Sales team is tasked with proficiently nurturing these leads within the CRM. By establishing shared objectives, the interconnectivity and mutual reliance of both systems are highlighted, fostering a sense of collective accountability and ensuring metric visibility throughout the connected systems.

Showcasing Success Stories

Sharing success stories regularly, where the coordinated use of all sales and marketing platforms leads to outstanding results, helps teams see tangible benefits in action. This increases their value perception and fosters a greater sense of ownership. For example, let's recall the trade show scenario highlighted earlier, which perfectly encapsulates the value of integrating these platforms.

Oren, the VP of Sales, alongside the Marketing team, meticulously prepared for a major trade show by leveraging both CRM and MAP capabilities. They identified key prospects likely to attend and launched targeted nurture campaigns, ensuring that Oren's interactions at the trade show were not just meetings but strategic engagements with well-informed potential clients.

Post-event, the quick follow-up strategy automated through the CRM allowed Oren to maintain momentum with the prospects, ensuring that each interaction they had with the company, whether at the trade show or through follow-up communications, was part of a coherent and personalized customer journey. This approach fortified the relationship between Sales and Marketing and highlighted the tangible benefits of CRM and MAP integration.

The most significant outcome was the biggest deal of the year, traced directly back to the leads nurtured and managed through this integrated system, exemplifying the immense value of these tools in action, fostering a greater appreciation and sense of ownership across both teams.

Empowering System Champions

Identifying and empowering system advocates or system champions within each team who excel in using the systems can also be beneficial. These individuals can serve as resources for others, providing tips, guidance, and encouragement. Their enthusiasm and expertise can help foster a culture that values and takes ownership of these tools.

In the trade show narrative featuring Oren, his role was crucial as the system champion. As the VP of Sales, Oren championed the idea that sales and marketing systems, while individual in their functions, should operate as a cohesive unit with specialized segments.

Oren's leadership went beyond Sales and Marketing cohesion. He actively demonstrated that the CRM and MAP, when integrated, could significantly enhance business outcomes. His strategy involved intertwining the strengths of both systems to create a unified approach.

For example, Oren's preparation for the trade show was a strategic blend of sales acumen and marketing insights. Each Sales interaction was informed and enriched by Marketing's data, ensuring a seamless customer journey. Oren's approach ensured that every interaction, from the initial email to the post-event follow-up, was part of a cohesive strategy.

Oren's advocacy as a system champion was impactful. He led by example, showcasing operational excellence through system integration. He inspired his teams to see sales and marketing functions as complementary parts of a single mechanism, aimed at achieving collective goals. This perspective nurtured a culture of collaboration and innovation, where success in one segment enhanced the overall performance, steering the organization toward collective achievements.

Feedback and Continuous Improvement

Establishing a feedback mechanism where Sales and Marketing can regularly offer suggestions for each other's systems can transform the way these teams interact and operate. This continuous improvement loop upgrades the systems' functionality and also fosters a sense of joint ownership and responsibility.

Imagine a scenario where the Marketing team launches a new digital advertising campaign. They use the MAP to track engagement metrics but might not have direct insights into how these leads perform once passed on to Sales. By establishing a feedback loop, Sales can provide real-time input on the quality of leads from the campaign, informing Marketing of the leads' status in the sales funnel and suggesting adjustments for targeting criteria or messaging.

Similarly, the Sales team, utilizing the CRM, can offer insights into the customer journey post-conversion. Feedback from Sales regarding customer queries or concerns can help Marketing tailor content or tweak strategies to address these areas, enhancing the overall customer experience and potentially increasing customer retention rates.

This mechanism could be as simple as a biweekly meeting or the shared digital platforms mentioned earlier, where both teams log insights, challenges, and suggestions. Over time, this collaboration can lead to refined marketing strategies that generate higher-quality leads and a sales approach that's more aligned with the customer's needs and expectations, thus ensuring both teams have a stake in the system's continuous development and improvement.

Visibility Across Integrated Systems

It is important that the CRM and MAP integrate in a way that is highly visible to both teams. When Sales and Marketing can directly observe how their actions in one system impact the other, it reinforces the notion of a unified, interconnected workflow, enhancing the sense of joint ownership.

Visible integration between CRM and MAP can be fostered through dashboards that display real-time data from both systems. These dashboards can be configured to show metrics that are relevant to both Sales and Marketing, such as the number of leads at each stage of the funnel, the average lead response time, or the conversion rates of specific campaigns. When these metrics are made visible to all relevant stakeholders, it converts abstract data into actionable insights.

Creating a common interface where both Sales and Marketing can track the customer journey from initial contact to closed sale eliminates the "black box" effect where efforts and outcomes are obscured between departments. This shared view promotes a culture of transparency and accountability.

Additionally, as mentioned in the Communications chapters, regular interdepartmental meetings where Sales and Marketing can discuss the insights gained from these systems help in aligning strategies and tactics. In these sessions, the teams can identify trends, discuss what is working and what isn't, and make data-driven decisions together.

This kind of integration also means that each team becomes more knowledgeable about the other's work. Marketing team members gain a better understanding of the sales cycle, while Sales can appreciate the depth of analysis that goes into targeting and nurturing leads. This cross-functional education enhances team collaboration and also builds a more resilient organization where members can step into different roles when needed.

Building a One-System Mindset

Let's reflect on the crucial actions and mindsets that are pivotal for harmonizing the efforts of Sales and Marketing.

The system's role extends beyond the technicalities of CRM and MAP tools; it's about people, their contributions, and the collaborative spirit they foster. The CASH framework, which underpins this book, thrives on the interdependence between Sales and Marketing and the components of the system itself.

Central to this interdependence is co-ownership. When both teams take ownership of the tools, the data they input, and the results they generate, the system functions optimally. Collaborative system customization is where this co-ownership can flourish. It includes working together to tweak features and then going further to shape a system that reflects the collective wisdom and objectives of both teams.

Cross-team training initiatives are another cornerstone. They bridge knowledge gaps and build a shared understanding, which is essential for the system's success. Training demystifies each team's tools, fostering a sense of familiarity and collective responsibility.

Creating cohesive performance metrics is equally important. Metrics should reach beyond individual team performance and demonstrate how both teams move the company forward together. These metrics serve as a common language, illustrating how aligned efforts contribute to the company's success.

Sharing success stories serves as powerful testimony to the benefits of a unified system. When teams hear how their combined efforts lead to tangible results, it reinforces their sense of shared ownership and commitment.

Empowering system champions within each team can catalyze this sense of ownership. These champions embody the collaborative spirit and drive continuous improvement.

Feedback and continuous improvement ensure the system remains dynamic and responsive to both teams' needs. This open channel for suggestions and improvements keeps the system evolving in line with Sales and Marketing's growing sophistication.

Visibility across integrated systems is the final piece of the puzzle. When teams can see the direct impact of their work on shared dashboards, it reinforces the interconnected nature of their roles and the importance of their collaboration.

In concluding this chapter, I emphasize that the system's role in alignment is multifaceted and dynamic. It's built on the foundation of co-ownership, mutual understanding, and continuous evolution. By taking the actions outlined in this chapter, Sales and Marketing can align their strategies and forge a partnership that drives the company's growth and success.

Chapter 11

Skin in the Game

While the phrase "skin in the game" may not translate well across cultures, it is a term widely used to define one's personal stake in the outcome of a situation. In other words, do you have sufficient investment or risk committed to ensure that your actions remain in line with seeking a successful outcome? When you have skin in the game, you have something to lose if things don't go well.

In regard to business, it's clear what the desired Sales outcomes are—more closed deals. To this effect, Marketing knows that if no deals get closed and revenues drop, the negative internal effects will more likely be felt by Marketing than the Sales team. Marketing has everything to lose if a company doesn't close deals, and they have no one to blame. If we argue that most of the customers' journey happens between the customers and their interactions with Marketing, then marketers have even fewer places to point fingers.

For this reason, marketers must be concerned with every lead. From the moment that lead hovers above the funnel, all the way through the funnel, and into the "customer delight" phase. Even beyond, when the customer considers a repeat purchase. Marketing, by nature, must have skin in the game from beginning to end.

Sales, on the other hand, can blame Marketing when fewer deals close. They can point to the pipeline shrinking, less qualified leads, less demand being generated, and lack of assistance in educating customers. However, this raises the question: Does Sales have skin in the game when it comes to Marketing outcomes?

The truth of the matter (and the reason this book exists) is that Sales often fails to share the responsibility of Marketing. Even though Sales is the recipient of Marketing's success, too often they don't see their responsibility to contribute to that success. So how do you get Sales to put some skin in the game of Marketing success?

Putting Sales Skin in the Marketing Game

To effectively engage Sales teams in marketing activities, where their contribution directly influences Marketing's success, we can focus on specific strategies and illustrate the implications of Sales' involvement—or lack thereof.

Case Study Development

Involving Sales team members in creating detailed case studies can significantly boost Marketing's efforts. When a salesperson contributes insights on how a deal was closed, including the challenges faced and how the product or service provided a solution, these real-world examples become powerful marketing tools. A well-documented case study can reveal Sales' contributions while showcasing the direct impact of Sales' involvement in Marketing's success. Conversely, a Sales team that doesn't contribute misses the opportunity to highlight successes that could have been used to attract similar clients. Involving Sales in case study development also directly affects the company's revenue generation. The process documentation leading to the case study allows a business to recognize successful patterns that can be repeated moving forward.

As we talk about case study development, let's not miss the importance of the word "development" here. Case study development should mean that Marketing is being inquisitive after the deal is closed and follows the customer to monitor success. Asking Sales how the customer launched, evolved, and succeeded is the center of a good case study. But waiting until the end makes it more difficult to gather the information. Sales and Marketing should work on this together, compiling information as the customer experiences the product.

Content Creation Collaboration

Sales teams possess firsthand insights into customer pain points and preferences. By collaborating with Marketing on content creation such as blog posts, podcasts, and videos, they can ensure that the content addresses real customer needs and interests. This targeted content is more likely to resonate with prospects, leading to higher engagement and conversion rates. A Sales team member's failure to contribute can result in less relevant content, diminishing their effectiveness and potentially leading to missed opportunities for lead generation.

Now you might ask, "How do you get a salesperson to stop selling and help create content?" You don't. You explain that you are going to create sales-enablement tools based on their knowledge and expertise. Then you interview them (preferably on camera) and ask all the questions that the customer would ask. This way, you have content in the exact words they would use to communicate with the customer. Sales is typically better at this than Marketing because Sales members would have had face-to-face encounters and talked to actual people rather than personas.

Another approach is to simply attend Sales' meetings and create content ideas based on the conversations you hear. As mentioned earlier, you will gain access to the customer objections and other angles that Sales has to address to move the customer toward a deal.

Social Selling Initiatives

Sales professionals can amplify marketing campaigns by sharing and promoting content through their personal and professional networks, especially on platforms like LinkedIn. This extends the reach of marketing efforts while lending credibility to the message. Sales team members who actively participate in social selling can trace increased engagement and leads back to their efforts. On the other hand, those who remain on the sidelines may find themselves disconnected from a valuable lead generation stream, impacting their potential to close deals.

Another important angle of social selling is how the customer perceives being approached. Is it a social approach, where giving and informing is the beginning of the relationship? Or is it a thinly veiled "ask" at the start of the encounter? When being social is the initial engagement, the selling becomes easier when the time comes. This is where even Sales can benefit from a Gary Vaynerchuk–style "Jab, Jab, Jab, Right Hook." In other words, "Give, give, give--then ask."

Feedback Loops for Campaign Optimization

Sales teams are in a unique position to provide feedback on marketing campaigns, offering insights into what resonates with prospects and customers. This feedback can be crucial for optimizing future marketing efforts. While rarely immediate, salespeople who actively contribute to this process will see a direct correlation between their feedback and improved marketing outcomes. These improved marketing outcomes lead to more qualified leads—exactly what Sales is asking for. Lack of involvement from Sales can result in missed opportunities for optimization, potentially leading to less effective marketing strategies that miss the targeted audience or provide leads unqualified for Sales.

Joint Participation in Events and Webinars

When Sales team members participate in marketing events and webinars, either as speakers or by engaging with attendees, they add a practical, real-world perspective that can enhance the event's value. Their involvement at this stage is not to sell but to be the trusted advisor in the room. This direct involvement allows Sales to share their expertise and form connections that can be nurtured into future opportunities. Sales professionals who ignore these opportunities miss the chance to build early customer relationships, establish themselves as a trusted advisor to the customer, and kick off a customer relationship in a low-pressure interactive environment.

Lead-Nurturing Programs

Sales teams can play a crucial role in designing and executing lead-nurturing programs. By sharing insights on the types of content that resonated with prospects at different stages of the buying journey, Sales can help tailor more effective nurturing sequences. If Sales teams are not involved, it makes Marketing's job of building a customer journey more difficult. We've established that the customer journey belongs to the customer. However, that doesn't mean Sales and Marketing should not work together to lay down a path for the customer to take. Sales insights help Marketing build the most direct path to a deal.

Customer Insight Collection for Product Development

Sales teams are on the front lines with customers and can provide valuable feedback to Marketing and Product Development teams regarding customer needs, preferences, and feature requests. This collaboration can inform product marketing strategies and help in the development of products that meet market demands more accurately. Without sufficient Sales involvement, Marketing and Product Development may lack critical customer insights, leading to less market-aligned product improvements or innovations.

Market Intelligence Sharing

Sales teams often gain insightful competitive intelligence on market trends through their interactions with prospects and customers. They may see trends appearing in customer behavior, questions, or interest in competing products. Sharing this information with Marketing can help adjust strategies, messages, and campaigns to better align with market dynamics and customer expectations. If Sales does not share these insights, marketing efforts may be based on outdated or incomplete information, potentially leading to less effective positioning against competitors.

Customer Success Stories and Testimonials

Collaborating with Sales to identify and document customer success stories and testimonials is another area where Sales involvement can directly impact Marketing's success. Sales professionals, being closer to customers, can pinpoint which clients have experienced significant success with the product or service.

Sales also understands the timing needed to ask a customer for a testimonial. For example, you don't want to ask for a testimonial if the customer is having issues with service or has product complaints. Perhaps you are in negotiation for contract renewal—this is another case where asking for a testimonial is bad timing or in poor taste. Sales can facilitate timing and introductions for Marketing to gather these testimonials. Lack of Sales' involvement here could mean creating a negative impression on the customer, leading to missed opportunities to capture compelling stories that can significantly boost credibility and attract potential customers.

Sales Enablement of Content Creation

Sales teams can inform the development of sales-enablement materials such as web pages, presentations, video, audio, infographics, and comparison documents, ensuring they're equipped with content that speaks directly to customer needs and objections encountered during the sales process. If Sales is not involved enough, Marketing might produce materials that are off target, not fully addressing the questions and concerns of prospects, thus hindering the efficiency and effectiveness of Sales.

In each of these activities, the contribution of Sales is measurable and directly tied to Marketing's success. Sales team members stand to gain significantly from being involved, with their efforts leading to more personalized and effective marketing strategies, ultimately resulting in increased lead generation and sales. Conversely, their lack of involvement can lead to missed opportunities, less effective marketing efforts, and, ultimately, a negative impact on their own sales performance.

Expert Insight—Joe Pulizzi

Joe Pulizzi shares additional insight on how a salesperson can become the trusted advisor to the customer while helping marketing efforts through content marketing:

As a salesperson, I want to be the trusted expert for my customer. We know that if we want to be the leading informational expert to our customer base, we have to deliver valuable, relevant, and compelling information to them on a consistent basis. My attitude is, "Wow, when my customers have a problem, they want to come to me!" A lot of salespeople don't think about it that way. I've been in sales almost 30 years now, and as a salesperson, I really do believe that if I present myself as not necessarily a solution that is a product or a service, but as a resource for them—that's going to position me above all other salespeople out there.

That's why I believe in content marketing and that it works so well, because I want to give all those answers, whereas you have some other people out there that want to hold onto that information. They say, "Oh, I can't give that all out because then my customers will do it themselves or they'll take that information and go somewhere else."

My response to that is, "That's my competitive advantage—giving everything away that I can possibly think of for free." And if some of those people take that information and go somewhere else, fine. Because most of those people don't want to do that.

They say, "I have this problem. Who can I think of that can help? Oh, it's the person that's been sending me this email newsletter for the last year and a half. It's the person that's been sending me this print magazine every quarter for the last two years. That company, that individual, I want to go to them." So it's funny when you think about it; even with an email newsletter, I don't ever expect to get a sale immediately when it comes to somebody signing up for a newsletter. I'm thinking, "This is a nice six- to twelve-month journey where I can build a relationship with that customer over a long period of time." Then the customers start to open this thing up.

The customers start to figure out, "This is something where I'm getting a lot of ongoing value." And then when they are ready to buy, they only think about me, or they only think about us as a company. And once a salesperson understands that when you give this stuff away you actually position yourself as the leading expert instead of holding it back. They understand that's why you have to look at [it] as, "Oh, I should be sharing this stuff on my LinkedIn channel. I should have an email newsletter. I should be sending my customers information that's going to help them live a better life in some way, help them get a better job in some way." If you strategically think about that, you're never going to have a problem selling stuff.

Incentives to Sales to Support Marketing

To ensure Sales teams see their effect on marketing success and are encouraged to participate in the described ways, incorporating specific incentives into the system is essential. Here are tailored incentives designed to motivate Sales teams to engage deeply with marketing activities.

Performance Dashboards

Develop comprehensive dashboards within the CRM or sales and marketing platforms that visually represent the direct impact of Sales activities on Marketing outcomes. These dashboards can highlight metrics such as lead conversion rates, engagement scores from sales-initiated interactions, and the revenue impact of collaborative sales and marketing campaigns. By making these metrics visible, Sales teams can see the tangible outcomes of their efforts, fostering a sense of accomplishment and motivation.

Recognition Programs

Implement recognition programs that publicly acknowledge the contributions of Sales team members to Marketing's success. This could include "Sales Contributor of the Month" awards based on metrics such as the number of high-quality leads generated from sales insights or the success rate of sales-driven marketing campaigns. Recognition provides a sense of pride and incentivizes continued contribution.

Commission and Bonus Structures

Adjust commission and bonus structures to include specific targets related to marketing engagement and collaboration. For instance, bonuses could be tied to the number of successful marketing campaigns based on the Sales team's contributed insights. Another tie-in could be the achievement of joint sales and marketing objectives such as content creation. These direct financial incentives encourage Sales teams to prioritize collaboration with Marketing.

Professional Development Opportunities

Offer professional development opportunities, such as advanced sales or marketing training and workshops, as rewards for active participation in marketing initiatives. Smart salespeople understand that they are better at their job if they understand Marketing Operations. (If they don't, give them a copy of this book.) Access to these learning opportunities can be seen as both a reward and an investment in the salesperson's career, encouraging them to engage more deeply with marketing efforts.

Cross-Functional Team-Building Events

Organize team-building events that mix Sales and Marketing teams, with participation tied to engagement in cross-functional activities. These events help build stronger personal connections between teams while creating a sense of collaboration. The CASH workshop is an example of this type of activity. It is an event designed for both Sales and Marketing professionals to learn together. Monthly events or annual sales kick-offs are ideal for this type of joint training.

Access to Exclusive Tools and Resources

Provide Sales team members who actively contribute to marketing efforts access to exclusive tools, resources, and software enhancements. This could include advanced CRM features, marketing automation tools, and premium content resources. As video becomes increasingly vital to the salesperson's toolbox, providing salespeople with tools and training to create videos will empower them to create content on their own. They will appreciate the autonomy to communicate with prospective customers and they will also gain respect for the work Marketing does in content creation. Access to these tools serves as an incentive and also empowers Sales teams to perform their roles more effectively.

Shared-Success Metrics

Integrate shared-success metrics into the incentive structure where both Sales and Marketing teams are rewarded for achieving common goals.

This approach ensures that both teams are aligned toward shared objectives, with incentives designed to foster collaboration and mutual support.

Incorporating these incentives into the system motivates Sales teams to engage in Marketing's activities and highlights the interdependent relationship between Sales and Marketing. By making the path from lead to opportunity transparent, and by rewarding collaboration, organizations can foster a culture where Sales and Marketing work together seamlessly, driving overall business success.

Chapter 12

Cohesive Sales and Marketing Reporting

The Psychology of Reports

Imagine a conference room full of salespeople and marketers. A Marketing member stands up to present their slides of marketing charts and reports. At that very moment, the Sales team members will take one of two positions:

1. "What on this screen will help me sell more?"

Or:

2. "What on this screen reflects my efforts?"

The members of the Sales team want to know if and how any of that information affects them. Now, being that it is about marketing—yes, it all has an effect on Sales, no matter whether the information is good or bad. What's important is that the person creating the report, in this case the marketer, has carefully thought out how the data will be received by their Sales counterparts and how to present the data in a way that makes Sales lean in.

Every marketing report—no matter if it is pre-funnel, top of the funnel, outside the funnel, or just fluffy social media marketing data—must aim to reflect how that effort will affect the company's overall sales strategy. This could be as simple as adding one more column to a report that Sales can relate to.

For example, a social media report that otherwise would be uninteresting to the Sales team may suddenly be worth gold if you add one column that indicates whether or not this social interaction was with a current customer. Even better yet—what if that social interaction was with a prospect in the salesperson's pipeline? Now you've turned a soft marketing report into something that shows Marketing's influence on the pipeline.

Another tactic that plays into the psychology of the Sales team comes down to words and titles. You can alter the perception of a report by simply renaming it. Changing a report name from "Social Influence Report" to "Pipeline Influence by Social" squarely places the report in the face of a salesperson worried about their pipeline. Words like "social," "influence," etc., mean nothing to the salesperson—but "pipeline," that's a word they may have recently caught heat over in a sales meeting. It means something.

Aside from altering Marketing reports to be more appealing for Sales, marketers should also seek to inject marketing attributes (data) into Sales reports—specifically, the reports that Sales regularly runs and reviews. Look for reports the Sales team already trusts, are already on their sales report dashboards, or are required submissions to their leaders. Then look for small ways to add a column or data point related to marketing.

For example, suppose there is a monthly report showing sales accepted leads (SALs). These are leads that Sales has deemed worthy of working on or that meet the criteria for being a potential customer. What marketing data might be useful to a Sales viewer of this report? Perhaps data such as a lead score to help them prioritize their outreach. Maybe the most recent marketing touches, such as how recently a prospect visited the website, what event the prospect attended, or what content the prospect consumed.

All these things can be positioned as a discrete addition to a Sales report without screaming out that they are from Marketing. You'll learn what data works because as soon as a data point is missing (as occurs with data), the salespeople will ask about it. That is a sure sign that the information is useful to them and that you have successfully injected useful marketing data into their Sales reports.

It's important to note that in order for a Marketer to begin doing these things, they will need to have a close relationship with Sales Operations or, even better, have sufficient rights to the CRM that Sales is using. In some organizations, sales reporting and CRM access are reserved for an elite few; however, after reading this book, you'll be able to better speak their language, understand their needs, and work your way into the ranks.

I have served in roles of Sales Operations (responsible for the CRM) and Marketing Operations (responsible for the MAP) and, at times, both of those at once. Being able to navigate through Sales Operations and Marketing Operations teams effectively requires you to understand what is important to both Sales and Marketing teams. It requires a deep understanding of how to present data that is actionable and that they can pass up through the executive ladder with confidence.

Gaining the Trust of Sales Report Gatekeepers

If you live solely in the Marketing team, here are a few tips to help you gain trust with the Sales team and Sales Operations in order to have greater influence on, or at least access to, the Sales reports.

Build Relationships through Regular Communication

Establish a regular cadence of meetings or check-ins with Sales Operations to stay informed and build a partnership. During these meetings, Marketing Operations can explore how they can support Sales' goals with marketing data. This regular dialogue helps identify what specific data points are valuable to Sales and ensures that Marketing's efforts are aligned with Sales' strategies. It can also serve as a platform to educate Sales on new marketing initiatives and technology while discussing how both teams can benefit from shared information.

Demonstrate Value with Data

One of the most compelling ways to showcase the importance of marketing value is through concrete data. By presenting case studies or specific examples of marketing initiatives that have led to sales, Marketing can clearly demonstrate their impact on the bottom line. This evidence should highlight the correlation between marketing activities and customer conversions or deal closures. This type of data underscores the value of marketing efforts and also builds a case for why Sales should pay attention to and incorporate Marketing reports into their operations.

Create Joint Goals

Collaboration thrives on shared objectives. When Marketing and Sales establish joint goals, such as a collective pipeline target or a mutual conversion metric, it aligns both teams toward a common purpose. These shared goals also provide a tangible reason for Sales to seek out and use marketing data, as it directly relates to achieving these objectives.

Furthermore, these collaborative targets encourage both teams to work together rather than in silos, fostering a more unified approach to the company's sales and marketing strategies. Note: "Unified" does not mean "uniformity." Each team has specific skills and tasks. Each person has unique skills and abilities. Yet they all must unify those assets to work for one common operational goal.

Offer to Assist with Analysis

Sales Operations often has a vast amount of data to process and analyze. By offering to assist with this analysis, Marketing can help to alleviate some of this workload while enriching the data by injecting marketing insights into the process. For instance, Marketing can provide a deeper understanding of customer behavior through engagement metrics or campaign responses. Offering this support showcases the value of marketing data and also puts Marketing in a position where their insights are seen as an integral part of the sales process.

Leverage CRM Insights

Marketing personnel with access to the customer relationship management (CRM) system have the opportunity to leverage its data to provide
valuable insights to the Sales team. Marketing can use CRM data to
segment leads based on their interaction with marketing materials and
prior purchases. This gives a broader picture of the customer journey
and helps to identify potential upsell opportunities. This segmentation
can also help Sales prioritize their efforts and tailor their approach to
different buyer groups, thereby increasing the efficiency and effectiveness
of their sales strategies.

Provide Customized Reporting

Designing and customizing reports for clear analysis and understanding
is key. By offering to create reports tailored to the needs of individual
salespeople, Marketing can ensure the data they provide is directly relevant
to each salesperson's pipeline. This makes the reports more useful and
shows the Sales team that Marketing understands their unique challenges
and is willing to provide bespoke support to help Sales succeed.

Educate on Marketing Metrics

There can often be a disconnect between Sales and Marketing due to a
lack of understanding of each other's metrics. By conducting educational
sessions on marketing metrics and how they relate to sales performance,
Marketing can bridge this gap. Such sessions can help Sales see the relevance of marketing data and how it can be used to enhance their work.
Education leads to appreciation, and once Sales understands the value
of marketing metrics, they are more likely to seek out this information
and incorporate it into their reports.

Advocate for Technology Integration

Marketing Operations professionals should champion the integration
of CRM and marketing automation platforms. This integration ensures
a seamless flow of data between Sales and Marketing, making it easier
for both teams to access the information they need when they need it.

Moreover, when Sales teams can see the direct impact of marketing activities within their own tools and systems, they are more likely to understand and value the contribution of Marketing to their efforts. Advocating for technology integration improves the efficiency of both teams while building a stronger case for the inclusion of marketing data in Sales Operations.

Sales Data in Marketing Reports

In most organizations, getting Sales data integrated into Marketing reports is a much smaller feat than the other way around. Any good marketing automation platform will be designed and expected to receive sales data. Also, the gatekeepers to Marketing Operations are much more welcoming than Sales Operations or CRM operators. That being said, cooperation with the Sales Operations is still valuable, if not absolutely required, in gaining access to the needed data.

In the symbiotic relationship between Sales and Marketing, the flow of data should be bidirectional to ensure both departments are aligned and informed. The inclusion of sales data in marketing reports is crucial for several reasons, which, when understood and acted upon, can significantly enhance the effectiveness of a company's overall revenue strategy.

Sales data provides tangible evidence of how marketing efforts are translating into actual revenue which is the lifeblood of any business. By incorporating sales figures, conversion rates, and customer acquisition costs (CACs) into marketing reports, marketers can gain a clear understanding of their return on investment (ROI). It is impossible to know if the customer acquisition cost is reasonable if you don't know the value of revenue it led to. If it costs $1,000 to acquire a $1 million customer, it's absolutely worth it! If that customer data reveals they are only worth $1,500—probably not. Marketing cannot know this without the sales data located in the CRM.

As another example, if a marketing report indicates that a particular campaign has led to a high number of leads but the sales data shows a low conversion rate, marketers can investigate and then address potential disconnects in the sales funnel. Better yet, they can adjust their campaign strategy altogether.

Including sales data helps in refining marketing strategies. It allows marketers to see which products or services are selling best and which demographics are making purchases. This information can help target marketing efforts more effectively. For instance, if a report reveals that a certain age group is responsible for the majority of purchases of a product, Marketing can tailor its content and advertisements to appeal to that demographic specifically.

Sales data also plays a crucial role in customer retention strategies. By tracking repeat purchase rates within marketing reports, marketers can identify the success of loyalty programs and customer engagement initiatives. This could involve analyzing which special offers or loyalty rewards are leading to repeat sales, allowing marketers to optimize these programs.

Furthermore, sales data can reveal trends and patterns that are invaluable for forecasting. If marketing reports include sales volume trends, marketers can adjust campaigns to anticipate seasonal fluctuations, market changes, or emerging consumer behaviors. For instance, if sales data within the marketing reports indicates an uptick in a particular product line during the summer months, Marketing can ramp up relevant promotional activities in the spring to maximize this seasonal trend.

Incorporating sales data into marketing reports also aids in aligning the two departments toward shared objectives. For example, if the goal is to increase market share in a specific region, marketing reports that include regional sales data can help both teams track progress and pivot strategies as needed.

Last, sales data in marketing reports can help in performance management and in providing incentives. When Marketing teams are able to see the direct results of their campaigns on sales figures, it can be a powerful motivator. Additionally, it provides a basis for setting KPIs and benchmarks for marketing performance that are directly tied to company revenue.

The inclusion of sales data in marketing reports is a strategic move that allows marketers to make data-driven decisions, demonstrate their impact on the company's bottom line, and foster a more collaborative and aligned relationship with the Sales team.

Effective and bidirectional reporting is also key between Sales and Marketing. It provides a complete picture of the customer journey and full-sighted business metrics, helping both teams see the bigger picture. This kind of reporting highlights Marketing's role in the sales cycle and encourages teamwork toward common objectives while promoting a culture driven by data.

This is a clear example of the described system where people, processes, and tools work together. Integrated reporting stands out as the crucial element that boosts decision-making across departments. It fosters feedback and improves processes, making sure Sales and Marketing's efforts are perfectly aligned to drive growth and revenue forward together with a clear strategy.

Chapter 13

Continuity Between Activities

How Systems and Terminology Work Against the Customer Journey

Within a few days of starting my new job as Global Digital Marketing Manager for a tech firm, I found myself baffled by how isolated the Sales Operations and Marketing Operations teams were from each other. I use the word "team" lightly here because I was basically the only member tasked with Marketing Operations. Sales not only had several employees working in Sales Operations, but also even an office and hierarchy for it.

When I asked questions about access to Salesforce, my marketing management responded as if I had asked for the password to the CEO's bank account! Salesforce wasn't something the Marketing department had access to. I had been a marketer and Salesforce administrator for the previous nine years, so a wall between Sales and Marketing was foreign to me. I expected that as the person in charge of the Marketing Operations platform, I would have access to the connected CRM. In this organization, this was far from the norm.

What was also far from the norm was a marketer who spoke "sales." And not just sales from a salesperson standpoint, but sales from a Sales Operations and technical perspective. I used their language—from the language Sales users spoke, down to the language the Salesforce programmers used. I could give them detailed examples of what I needed to connect between systems in a way that did not sound like a marketer. I even had screenshots and automation designs from instances I had previously built. Being able to talk the talk quickly made me an insider and member of the Sales Operations team.

While I was still relatively new to the company, I needed some changes made in Salesforce for better marketing integration. I was able to get it done with the help of Sales Operations within a couple of days. This type of task and request was usually received by Sales Ops with a lot of pushbacks and long delays or even completely brushed off.

I remember my manager saying something to the effect of, "How on earth did you get the Salesforce dev team to do that so quickly? It usually takes us months, if we get a response at all!" That was the moment it became very clear to me that there were organizational divisions that needed healing. This moment led me to seeing additional opportunities to bring Sales and Marketing together.

As I spent more time with the Sales Operations team, I gained a huge respect for their structure and how well they protected the integrity of the company's sales data. I also earned the team's respect as I began to challenge the practices and structure of the CRM. However, they had one major breakdown in their system that I was determined to fix.

Before I explain this particular breakdown, let me explain the situation that often causes this system breakdown between Sales and Marketing teams.

A common pitfall that becomes apparent upon closer inspection involves the inconsistent use of terminology across the Marketing, Sales, and Sales Operations when referring to potential customers at various stages of the sales process. This discrepancy arises from the fact that marketing automation platforms (MAPs) and customer relationship management (CRM) systems often label potential customers with different terms.

For example, what one system might call a "Prospect," another might label as a "Lead," "Contact," or even "Person." Such variations in nomenclature can lead to confusion as the same individual might be referred to differently across systems like Salesforce, Pardot, Marketo, HubSpot, and Oracle Eloqua, to name a few I've personally had my hands in.

This inconsistency might seem to be a minor inconvenience until you begin to properly connect your systems. It easily becomes a major inconvenience because it represents a significant barrier to effective communication and process flow between Sales and Marketing teams. When a "Lead" in a CRM does not align with the same concept in a MAP, communication breakdowns begin. This lack of clarity can result in inefficiencies in lead management processes, challenges in accurately tracking the customer journey, and, ultimately, a disconnect in the alignment of sales and marketing strategies.

Challenges like these highlight the need for a unified system and well-planned integration between CRM systems and MAPs. It's important for every team member to understand the specific terms and their equivalents across platforms. Proper integration and comprehensive training on these terminologies can reduce confusion and promote a cohesive and effective approach to managing the customer life cycle. This seamless flow of information is essential for aligning Sales and Marketing efforts, which enhances the overall efficiency and effectiveness of business strategies. This is a topic that should be thoroughly discussed in shared operational meetings and shared system development, which we mentioned earlier.

Table 13.1 shows just how disruptive naming conventions can be when platforms are integrated into your system.

Table 13.1 Naming Conventions Across Platforms

System	Object Name	Equivalent Concept
Salesforce CRM	Lead	Potential customer
Salesforce CRM	Contact	Qualified individual
Marketo MAP	Lead	Individual in database
Pardot MAP	Prospect	Individual in database
HubSpot CRM/MAP	Contact	Interested individual
Microsoft Dynamics 365 CRM	Lead	Potential interest
Microsoft Dynamics 365 CRM	Contact	Closed or ongoing business individual
HubSpot Marketing Hub MAP	Contact	Individual engaged with company
Oracle Eloqua MAP	Contact	Individual engaged with marketing

This is only an example, based on some popular marketing and CRM platform structures at the moment. These are subject to change; however, the problem will likely persist. First, understand this exists, then work with your teams to make it clear how to communicate these terms. Then structure your systems to coordinate a smooth customer journey regardless of the customer labels or object names.

Now, back to the story.

I was brought into the picture to finish integrating the new Pardot instance with Salesforce. The initial phase of this process was disconnecting the Oracle Eloqua MAP that was connected to Salesforce. The first challenge was partly because of the confusing naming conventions and partly because of a lack of cohesiveness in operations. The problem was that the "Contacts" in Eloqua were connected to the "Contacts" in Salesforce, as if they were the same. This connection seems logical at the surface if you only go by names. However, a Contact in Eloqua is a new person that Marketing is still working on. That person is not sales-ready and should still be what Salesforce calls a "Lead." Fixing that was the first challenge revealed. At least in this case we were getting rid of Eloqua, so breaking this already broken connection was the least of my challenges.

Then I discovered that records from Eloqua were only sent to Salesforce when they reached a particular marketing qualification threshold. This meant that Sales had no view of marketing activity unless marketing pushed a record into Salesforce. That is a problem within itself. However, that action also began to unveil the most significant issue that I discovered.

When a person was pushed from the marketing platform to the Salesforce CRM, a completely new record was created! This record was void of marketing histories such as touchpoints, content consumed, and existing records of communication with the prospective customer. This issue was not truly uncovered until the Pardot instance was installed and we naturally and correctly associated Pardot Prospects with Salesforce Leads. Both of these person-related objects implied that these "people" were not necessarily sales-ready, but they needed to be visible to both Marketing and Sales from the start of their customer journey.

Remember, previously, Contacts from Eloqua became Contacts in Salesforce. Now the Sales Operations team has the new guy (me) filling up their CRM with Lead records—something they had not previously paid much attention to. With the implementation of these Lead records comes a new revelation . . . what happens when these Leads are ready to be addressed by Sales?

It was at this point that I suggested, as Salesforce is designed, to implement a process where the Leads flowing in from Pardot remain as Leads until they are accepted by Sales. (*Acronym alert:* This is known as a Sales accepted lead, or SAL.) At this point, they are converted to Contacts and ready to be connected to an Account.

This is where the big breakdown occurred:

It was revealed to me that, instead of converting the Lead into a Contact, a brand-new blank record was created as a Contact—as if they weren't the same person! My mind was blown!

I wasn't ready for that drastic of an example of how the customer journey could be severed . . . cut . . . thrown away. In this case, the process was literally starting from scratch with a new record, leaving behind marketing history and early sales efforts by inside sales. It took nearly a year to fix this situation, and by the time we did, we achieved a continuous view of the customer journey. I had also begun to build the case for creating a Marketing Operations team.

What Permissions Say About Cohesiveness

As a Marketer, I broke the norm, and possibly broke rank, by having the nerve to ask for advanced user permission in the CRM. By wearing both Marketing Operations and Sales Operations hats in previous positions, I naturally connected the two worlds as different branches of the same tree. This is not the case with many organizations. Your first clue to seeing if this is a problem in your organization comes from investigating who has permission to access what platforms. Obviously, there can be cost issues in terms of the number of user licenses involved. However, the pros far outweigh the cons when it comes to providing more access to users over less.

Permission structure within an organization is a clear indicator of the organization's approach to collaboration and cohesion between Sales and Marketing. When Marketing team members lack access to the CRM system and Sales personnel are not privy to data in the marketing automation platform, it sends a message about the disjointed nature of these departments. This separation hinders the fluid exchange of information. It derails the alignment of goals and strategies, which are crucial for unified business operations.

Limited permissions reveal a lot about an organization's culture and structure. It indicates a siloed approach where Sales and Marketing are seen as separate entities with little interaction instead of parts of a unified Revenue team. This division hinders effective communication, reduces data efficiency, and negatively impacts the customer experience. Investing in a few more user licenses is a small cost compared with the value of bridging this gap.

Granting cross-access to these systems can serve as a powerful statement of trust and mutual respect between Sales and Marketing. It acknowledges the intertwined nature of their work and the importance of each team's contributions to the company's success. More importantly, it facilitates a more integrated and cohesive strategy where insights are shared freely, strategies are developed collaboratively, and goals are aligned.

Access permissions are far more than the technical ability to log into a system; they are about empowering team members to search for and use the information they need to make informed decisions and take meaningful actions. When Marketing understands the nuances of Sales' interactions, and Sales can see the direct impact of Marketing's efforts, each team can perform their roles more effectively and with a greater sense of direction.

What permissions say about cohesiveness is significant. They either signal a commitment to integration and unity between Sales and Marketing or highlight a divide that could hamper the organization's ability to operate efficiently. For companies striving for revenue growth and competitiveness, aligning these permissions with the goal of collaboration is essential.

Chapter 14

The Future of the System

Automating business processes is one of my guilty (geeky) pleasures. While working in Sales Operations and Marketing Operations, it was a thrill to create systems that seemed to magically work on their own. The more complex a "if this, then that" scenario I could make, the more intelligent and more efficient the systems I managed seemed. As artificial intelligence (AI) began creeping into platforms (Salesforce's Einstein, for example), it became evident that complicated processes and deep analysis were something that could and should be built directly into business software.

AI is poised to further unify the Sales and Marketing strategies, enhancing collaboration and efficiency. By granting both teams access to shared data, AI enables more accurate targeting and campaign personalization through detailed analysis of customer behaviors and preferences. Looking ahead, AI will facilitate the creation of marketing content that resonates with customer needs while providing Sales teams with real-time insights, leading to better client interactions. This synergy will ensure a consistent and cohesive customer experience.

Additionally, AI will dismantle traditional silos, creating a more integrated environment. With a complete view of the customer journey, Marketing can tailor communications more effectively and Sales can fine-tune their strategies using precise data. This integration will not only boost the effectiveness of each team but also improve overall customer satisfaction, turning these functions into a cohesive, revenue-generating unit. AI's role in Sales and Marketing is set to expand, making their collaboration more seamless and impactful.

I left my last Marketing Operations job in 2022—the same year ChatGPT made AI available to all with an internet connection. As soon as I began challenging it with analysis and automation, I started thinking of the weeks, often months, I had spent in the past year raking through data to create reports and cross-reference Sales and Marketing information to make sense at a revenue level. Management questions could now be asked directly to AI, in natural language, in order to output the data that previously took days of report configuration to reveal.

It was at that moment I realized the job I just left would be changed forever. What took me weeks could now be done in minutes. I also realized that my experience in knowing what questions to ask made all the difference in how useful this AI would be.

What AI cannot change is the people using the systems.

At some level, people will always be responsible for asking the right questions of AI. Because people will (and should) be the primary architects of a business's strategy, they should also be the ones asking the questions regarding progress toward strategy success.

Salespeople still need to ask questions like, "What marketing efforts best support sales efforts to close deals?" "What sales tactics are the most effective?" and, "What sales activities lead to the most revenue, regardless of product?"

Marketing people still need to ask questions like, "What marketing activities drive the most pipeline?" "What customers do we target that lead to the most closed business?" and, "What sales activities need additional support from Marketing?"

These will increasingly be questions that AI can answer, but they must start with the questions from the strategy architects—the humans. In addition, when humans are taking actions, those actions must be documented electronically for AI to respond with usable answers. For example, the question, "What marketing efforts best support sales efforts to close deals?"—sure, AI can tell you that, based on its knowledge of marketing activities.

However, AI can only respond to what data has been input. In other words, if the humans do not input their activity into the system, AI will lack the data to be useful. AI is not having dinner meetings, playing golf with customers, or delivering word-of-mouth interactions—therefore, humans will still be a key to the system, even if not the center of it.

Because of the rapid evolution of AI as a tool in the system, artificial intelligence is not a subject that can be relegated to a static book; however, the underlying requirement of people and process will remain as long as people are the end users of business productivity.

If you are interested in my thoughts on AI and tech innovations as they apply to this subject, you'll need to subscribe to my newsletter at **ALeeJudge.com** and follow me on social platforms such as LinkedIn. I will be regularly sharing insights with you as AI evolves around Sales and Marketing.

Expert Insight—Sandy Carter

To close this short chapter, I want to again share the thoughts of Sandy Carter. I encourage you to check out her most recent books on AI, business, and Web3. Being that she is a pioneer in AI innovation as well as a seasoned executive leader, Sandy's views on the long-lasting effects of AI on Sales and Marketing are invaluable. Here are her thoughts:

There are some really interesting ways that are long lasting that Sales and Marketing can be assisted with AI. One of the biggest is lead scoring to help with prioritization. If you think about AI, if you train AI enough on what type of leads close, what type of decision-maker might make the close: Is it a developer? Is it the CTO, CIO, chief marketing officer? Where is that variable of closure happening fastest? Analyzing historic data. Analyzing engagement levels. I'm seeing a lot of examples of people using AI predictive analytics to score leads, then having that scoring drive marketing efforts so that they're driving their efforts toward the most valuable leads. Then the sales team can also prioritize their efforts on those prospects as well. I think that's one place that AI can really help out. It's not a specific tool, but it's more of the approach that I think will grow as well.

The other big example is personalized customer experience or engagement—using AI chatbots to engage with your website visitors in real time but providing personalized responses and then collecting that data. These new chatbots can almost qualify a lead, asking relevant questions like your lead specialist could do today, and then direct a high-quality lead to a sales rep. So, for me, creation of that chatbot and understanding the customer experience, understanding what that personalized engagement could be, would be a marketing task and then bridging the gap between Marketing and Sales.

THE FUTURE OF THE SYSTEM

Capturing and qualifying that lead—I think that's another great example I have seen people using.

I used to work for IBM, and one of the interesting things we did is use IBM Watson to analyze social media and customer reviews and use that data to gauge customer sentiment. So now we're not talking about acquiring a customer, we're talking about keeping a customer, a loyal customer. We're talking about analyzing and using that information for Marketing and Sales to refine their strategy.

Part 4

C
A
S
<u>H</u>onesty

Honesty doesn't always mean the opposite of a lie. And the absence of honesty does not mean there was an intent to be dishonest. However, when it comes to organizational collaboration—that is when culture, management structure, effort, and incentives can get in the way.

For Sales and Marketing teams, honesty means creating an environment where truthfulness thrives naturally. It's about ensuring everyone is on the same page, sharing accurate information, and working toward shared goals. The next few chapters explore how fostering honest relationships, maintaining transparency in reporting, and setting realistic goals can transform team dynamics. By embracing honesty, teams can build trust, enhance communication, and drive better results. Part 4 pulls back the layers of honesty in a business environment to discuss its critical role in aligning Sales and Marketing for cohesive and effective collaboration.

Chapter 15

Honest Relationships

The Rarest of Birds—the Bluebird

Here we are: Back at the boardroom table. A room full of Sales team members and a handful of marketers. The CEO is going from salesperson to salesperson, examining their deal pipeline for the week. Some are giving updates on the whale (the big deal) they are working hard to close. For others, it's about all the new relationships they have landed. And yet for others, it's about what objections or needs they must reply to in order to close a deal.

One salesperson proudly reported that his sales pipeline had been blessed with a "bluebird"—a new business opportunity that just fell out of the sky and into his lap.

This is where I, the young marketer, raised my hand.

The company he named, that just fell out of the sky, sounded very familiar. I had seen it many times in our attendee lists and form fills. I quickly pulled up the customer in the marketing automation platform. It turned out that the salesperson had entered a duplicate into the CRM—totally missing that a prospect record for the person was already there, synced over from the marketing automation platform.

As my hand raise was recognized, I respectfully proceeded to inform the room that this prospect had been in our sales pipeline for nearly two years. The prospect had attended several webinars, downloaded white papers, regularly opened our emails, and frequently visited our website. They were a prime example of how prospects take their own journey and don't contact Sales until they are ready to buy. The prospect was not a bluebird. They were a well-informed prospect in a long sales cycle and a self-directed customer journey.

After this meeting, I was left thinking:

> "What business opportunities were we close to getting but lost because Sales and Marketing weren't on the same page?
>
> "What other won opportunities like this have occurred, where Sales thought they brought in business all on their own?"
>
> "What business was attributed to one set of campaigns or events that was really the result of others?"
>
> "How much more effective would our business be if we worked together as a Revenue team rather than Sales and Marketing teams?"

It was a sign that the two teams had not been communicating sufficiently. They were not aligned in their strategies and, as a result, we weren't honest as an organization about where our leads and new business came from. We reported things that simply were not true.

Because Sales and Marketing happened to be in the same meeting, as prescribed in the Communication chapters in this book, the system data was revealed and kept us honest about where this new business came from. Luckily, Marketing was in the room to point this out—at least in this particular case.

Keeping Sales and Marketing Relationships Honest

In no way am I going to infer that salespeople or marketers will outright lie about their contributions to a company's revenue—though I'm sure some individuals are guilty. That is not directly the type of honesty we're talking about.

The honesty I refer to here is regarding the understanding and admission that very few deals close through the effort of one team only. Just like in the bluebird story, Sales did not attract the prospect alone, if at all. At the same time, Marketing didn't close the deal.

Perhaps Marketing could be more honest in the notion that, while they gather prospects based on demographics, psychographics, and sales history, they may not have the sales savvy to convince customers face-to-face to close a deal. For big corporate or business-to-business (B2B) deals, a lot of face time and negotiation is required. In these cases, a lot of work is to be done after bringing a deal to the table. Sales has to engage their unique skill sets to close the deal.

On the other side, Sales needs to understand that there is nearly no such thing as a bluebird. No one wakes up in the morning, has a light-bulb pop over their head and says, "Hey, I want to buy this product I've never heard of!" No—it doesn't work that way. Marketing has been in that customer's eyes, ears, and mind long before the customer reached out to a salesperson. Sales needs to be honest and open about that reality.

As a marketer who has always been determined to work closely with Sales, I was frequently put in a position to ask Sales to do things they may not have wanted to do. I once had a CEO who was a sales leader himself tell me that "salespeople are lazy." I don't think he meant that they literally lacked initiative or did not want to work; I'm confident what he meant was that if they don't see a straight line to results from their efforts, they're not going to make the effort.

This CEO had to be one of the most honest salespeople I've ever worked with. He taught me the most valuable lesson about working with salespeople: that Sales works off WIIFM, or "What's in It For Me." WIIFM, or "wiffem," was a term that was thrown around a lot. No matter how grandiose your sales campaign or your marketing initiative is, it will be nothing to the Sales team if they cannot see what's in it for them.

Being chosen to speak at an upcoming sales kickoff, I tackled the challenge head-on with the intention of getting the Sales team members to do something many of them did not want to do: Social selling. They had all been tasked with learning how to social-sell, but most had been flying under the radar and not taking it seriously nor reporting their activity honestly. So there I was, a marketer on stage in front of a room full of salespeople, talking about how to sell, and of all places on social media. Not their favorite place to do business.

As I looked across the room full of salespeople, there was nothing on their faces but the expression of "What's in it for me?" They were concerned with why this marketing guy was trying to convince them to take time out of their sales activities to create video for LinkedIn, create social posts, and communicate with clients on social media instead of email or the phone.

And then I put a slide up on the big screen. It was a conversation on LinkedIn that I had been having with the champion of the company's biggest client. We had several back-and-forth comments and the client was fully engaged in the conversation I was having about an industry topic. I looked over to the salesperson who owned that account and asked him, "Have you had this kind of conversation with our client recently?"

You should've seen the look on his face. I'm not sure if he was shocked that I was talking with his client or if he was surprised at how this marketer had more access to communicate with a top client than he did. Needless to say, from that point on, he and every other salesperson in the room leaned in to hear what this marketer had to say for the rest of the presentation.

As the presentation went on, I found out that there were at least two salespeople in the audience who had honestly bought into the idea of social selling and had quietly been using it as a secret weapon. Because they were perhaps not proud of doing things the nontraditional way, they had not admitted or shared that social selling was a part of their daily activity. This, by the way, was a cultural flaw of the company leadership, which the company was actively correcting by having me on stage.

Another element of honesty that was missing in the room was the fact that some of the salespeople honestly knew that social selling would help their bottom line; however, they weren't honest about the fact that they didn't know how to do it, and maybe even didn't want to. After this presentation, we were able to have an open conversation on the topic, train more Sales team members on social selling, and hash out the reasons why there were hesitancies and reservations about using social media.

Some admitted that they felt it was Marketing's job. At least they were honest.

Honesty to Management

At one time, I was the Salesforce CRM administrator as well as the leader of the Marketing team. This, oddly enough, placed me in a position where I had an indirect leadership role over the inside Sales team. This occurred because, just like Marketing, their job was to generate a volume of leads. We both had the goal of finding unknown prospects, pulling them into our funnel, and deciding who was worthy of being turned over to the Sales team.

While working closely with inside sales, I recognized that one of the team members kept a pile of yellow legal pads stashed in his desk drawer. This, by no coincidence, was the same team member whose work rarely showed up in Salesforce reporting. Being that we had adopted the mantra of "If it isn't in Salesforce, it didn't happen," a lot of his work "didn't happen." When I approached him with the intent of helping his Salesforce reports look more indicative of his hard work, he replied that he intentionally did not put information into Salesforce. He didn't want others to know what he was doing. He felt that keeping the information to himself was a protective act toward keeping his leads to himself.

The effect, however, was quite the opposite. In the end, others got credit for his work, he couldn't prove his work, and eventually he was let go. I don't know if he took his yellow note pads with him or not.

It wasn't that he was withholding truth from the organization, but that he wasn't honestly reporting his activities. Doing so would have been a benefit for both him and the company. And, evidently, the company chose to protect itself in the long run.

In a setting with defined Sales and Marketing roles, honesty is crucial for the success of the organization. And there are instances where Sales and Marketing teams might withhold information or not fully disclose the reality of situations to management. This behavior can be motivated by various factors.

Performance Pressure

When Sales and Marketing teams face the daunting task of meeting targets and quotas, there's a strong temptation to modify performance data or overstate the effectiveness of certain campaigns. This modification often stems from the fear of negative consequences such as criticism or job insecurity, which can be exacerbated in high-stress, high-expectation environments. Here honesty is more than a moral choice. It is a necessity that supports long-term success and credibility within the organization.

The erosion of trust between these teams and management can have far-reaching implications. When performance issues are masked, it hinders the organization's ability to respond effectively to market conditions. This also leads to a delay in necessary strategy adjustments that could have otherwise rectified underlying issues or unsuccessful initiatives. Moreover, this lack of transparency can foster a toxic work culture where short-term gains are prioritized over sustainable growth and employee well-being.

To counteract these pressures, organizations must foster an environment where honesty is valued and protected. This involves creating communication channels that encourage open dialogue without fear of consequences. Management should emphasize that honest reporting is more valuable than embellished results, as it provides a realistic picture of the market and the team's performance.

Additionally, implementing support systems such as realistic goal setting, regular feedback loops, and psychological safety can reduce the performance pressure that fuels dishonesty. By aligning incentives with honest and constructive reporting, companies can ensure that their teams are not motivated simply to meet targets but also to contribute to the organization's robust and ethical growth.

Fear of Consequences

The fear of negative consequences such as job loss, demotions, or other punitive actions can significantly impact the behavior of Sales and Marketing teams. This fear often drives teams to withhold information about failures or challenges such as unsuccessful campaigns, product launches, or a declining market share. Such behavior obscures the reality of the situation from management and also hampers the organization's ability to make informed decisions that could address and rectify these issues.

When teams feel threatened by the potential repercussions of failure, they may resort to presenting an overly optimistic view of their efforts and outcomes. This can create a distorted picture that leads to continued investment in unsuccessful strategies or products, wasting valuable resources and potentially missing opportunities to pivot or innovate in response to market demands.

To mitigate these fears, organizations should foster an environment that views failures and challenges as opportunities for learning and growth rather than causes for punishment.

This can be achieved through several strategies:

1. **Emphasizing Learning Over Blame:** Shift the focus from blaming individuals for failures to understanding what can be learned from these situations. Encourage teams to conduct thorough postmortem analyses on unsuccessful projects and share their findings without fear of retribution. This approach promotes a growth mindset and, importantly, enhances collective knowledge, making each team member feel valued and integral to the organization while reducing future mistakes.

2. **Rewarding Transparency:** Recognize and reward employees who demonstrate courage and integrity by being transparent about their challenges and failures. These rewards can shift the

organizational culture to one that values honesty and continuous improvement over ordinary success metrics.

3. **Setting Realistic Expectations:** Ensure that goals and targets are realistic and achievable. Unrealistic expectations can pressure teams to manipulate results or become disheartened by their inability to meet such goals.

4. **Providing Supportive Leadership:** Leaders should actively support their teams by providing the tools, resources, and guidance needed to succeed. When failures occur, leaders should step in to hold individuals accountable and to offer support and solutions to overcome these challenges.

5. **Promoting Open Communication:** Establish regular check-ins and feedback sessions where teams can discuss ongoing projects and potential red flags without fear. Intentional, open communication keeps everyone informed and engaged in finding solutions early before problems escalate.

By adopting these strategies, organizations can create a supportive culture that diminishes the fear of negative consequences and encourages a more honest, collaborative, and proactive workforce. This shift improves morale and drives more effective and innovative business practices, aligning teams toward common goals with a shared commitment to integrity and success.

Desire for Recognition or Advancement

The desire for recognition or advancement is a powerful motivator that can sometimes lead individuals or teams within Sales and Marketing to exaggerate successes or minimize setbacks. This drive to appear more competent or successful can stem from a pursuit of rewards such as bonuses, promotions, or simply the affirmation of one's skills and capabilities. While striving for recognition is natural and often beneficial, it becomes problematic when it fosters dishonesty or misrepresentation of the true performance metrics.

This behavior undermines individual credibility and hampers the organization's ability to accurately assess and respond to its actual performance. When successes are exaggerated, it can lead to strategic errors such as overinvesting in less fruitful initiatives or neglecting urgent areas because their issues have been downplayed.

To address these challenges and minimize their impact, organizations can implement several key strategies:

1. **Highlight the Positive Impact:** Organizations can recognize an employee's full contributions by creating systems that reward both end results and the integrity of the process, including efforts toward innovation and problem-solving. This approach, which emphasizes individual contributions to the bigger picture instead of just team reports, significantly reduces the incentive to misrepresent results.

2. **Set Clear Criteria for Advancement:** Establish clear, transparent criteria for promotions and bonuses that include qualitative and quantitative metrics. Ensure these criteria are well communicated and understood by all team members. This transparency helps mitigate misunderstandings about what is valued and reduces the temptation to game the system.

3. **Foster a Culture of Integrity:** Cultivate an organizational culture that places a high value on honesty and ethical behavior. Leaders should model these values by acknowledging their own setbacks and how they address them, thereby setting a precedent that failure is a part of the growth process and not to be hidden.

4. **Encourage Collaborative Team Dynamics:** Promote an environment where team success is celebrated alongside individual achievements. This can help to dilute the pressure on individuals to outshine at the expense of truth, fostering a more supportive and less competitive atmosphere.

5. **Provide Regular Training and Development:** Provide regular training on ethical behavior and the long-term benefits of integrity in professional life. Educational programs can reinforce

the importance of accurate reporting and transparency in building a sustainable career.

6. **Implement Robust Audit and Feedback Mechanisms:** Regular audits and checks on reported data can deter manipulation by increasing the likelihood of discovery. Feedback mechanisms that allow for anonymous reporting of unethical practices can also help maintain honesty within teams.

By instituting these measures, companies can encourage a more honest disclosure of successes and setbacks, thereby enhancing the decision-making process and aligning individual ambitions with the organization's long-term goals. This alignment helps to ensure that personal career advancement and recognition are achieved through genuine contributions, benefiting both the individual and the organization as a whole.

Cultural Issues

Cultural issues within an organization can significantly impact the honesty of its teams. In environments where there is a lack of open communication channels or a punitive approach to mistakes and failures, employees may feel compelled to hide or manipulate information. This is often done to align with the expected narratives or outcomes they believe management wants to hear. Such a culture discourages honesty and restricts innovation and growth by creating an atmosphere of fear and mistrust.

To combat these issues and foster a culture of honesty, management can take proactive steps to support open communication and a nonpunitive approach to mistakes.

Here's how management can effectively nurture such an environment:

1. **Promote Psychological Safety:** Management should work to create a psychologically safe workplace where employees feel secure enough to share ideas, ask questions, and report problems or failures without fear of embarrassment or retribution. This involves recognizing and addressing behaviors that undermine psychological safety, such as public criticism or dismissiveness.

2. **Establish Open Communication Channels:** Develop multiple channels for open and honest communication. This includes regular team meetings, one-on-one sessions with supervisors, anonymous feedback tools, and open-door policies that encourage direct interaction with higher management. These channels should be actively promoted and genuinely valued by leadership.

3. **Normalize the Discussion of Failures:** Management can change the organizational perception of failure by openly discussing their own mistakes and the lessons learned from them. Highlighting case studies within the company where failures led to important insights or business pivots can also help in normalizing such discussions.

4. **Implement Restorative Approaches to Mistakes:** Instead of punitive measures, adopt a restorative approach that focuses on understanding what went wrong and why without assigning blame. Use mistakes as learning opportunities that contribute to personal and organizational growth. This approach encourages employees to be up front about setbacks and collaborate on solutions.

5. **Train Leaders to Encourage Honesty:** Provide training for managers and team leaders on how to encourage honesty and handle disclosures of mistakes or failures constructively. They should be equipped with skills to handle such conversations sensitively, ensuring the focus remains on constructive outcomes rather than punitive actions.

6. **Recognize and Reward Transparency:** Actively acknowledge and reward behaviors that demonstrate transparency and honesty. This could be through formal recognition programs or simply verbal acknowledgment in meetings. Making transparency a recognized and rewarded value reinforces its importance in the organizational culture.

7. **Audit and Adjust Policies:** Regularly review company policies and management practices to ensure they support rather than hinder transparency. This could involve adjusting performance

metrics, reevaluating target settings, and revising any systems that may inadvertently encourage manipulating data or hiding information.

By implementing these strategies, management can effectively support a culture of honesty. This supportive environment enhances trust and cooperation across the organization and drives better decision-making and adaptability, which are crucial for long-term success in a dynamic business landscape.

Competitive Dynamics

Just like our inside salesperson who hoarded information on yellow legal pads in his desk drawer, team members may similarly withhold crucial data to secure a perceived advantage over their colleagues. This mindset can lead to siloed knowledge, where information about pipeline status, competitive threats, or market changes is not shared freely within the team or with management. The fear of being blamed for not responding adequately or swiftly enough to market dynamics can further exacerbate this issue, stifling communication and hindering a cohesive strategic response.

To mitigate these detrimental dynamics, organizations must cultivate a culture grounded in trust and open communication.

This involves several proactive steps:

1. **Encourage Regular Updates and Check-Ins:** Organizations should foster an environment where regular updates and check-ins are standard practice. These meetings should track progress and also provide a forum for discussing challenges and setbacks openly. Establishing this regular rhythm of communication helps to break down the barriers that hoarding information creates, ensuring that all team members are well informed and can collaboratively respond to market changes and internal dynamics. See the Communication chapters.

2. **Provide Safe Spaces for Reporting Challenges:** Implementing anonymous feedback tools, regular one-on-one check-ins with managers, and team sessions explicitly framed as judgment-free

zones to discuss what is not working are crucial. These platforms must be genuinely supportive and free from repercussions to encourage honesty and vulnerability from team members.

3. **Implement Realistic Goal Setting:** Goals should be challenging yet achievable and emphasize team performance over individual accomplishments. This approach helps to dilute the competitive nature of work environments and aligns team members toward common objectives, fostering a sense of unity and shared purpose.

By integrating these strategies, companies can ensure that Sales and Marketing teams align more closely with ethical practices and work cohesively toward achieving organizational objectives. This environment supports the strategic goals of the company as well as contributes to a more engaged and motivated workforce.

Expert Insight—Laura Erdem

Laura Erdem is a sales leader and social selling expert who gained prominence through her innovative work at Dreamdata, a B2B SaaS platform specializing in revenue attribution. Throughout her career, Laura has established herself as a thought leader in Sales and Marketing alignment. She is known for her strategic use of LinkedIn for inbound lead generation and her approach to social selling has influenced countless professionals in the B2B tech industry.

I asked Laura for her view on maintaining honesty in reporting while managing expectations of credit given to the effort contributed from Sales or Marketing teams. She suggests a strategy of focusing on the data rather than the two teams:

This is a job for the Operations team. It is not Marketing's or Sales' job, because as soon as we put one or the other in charge of giving credit to something, you know where the credit is going. There is a reason why operations is a key function within the company: Because somebody has to own the data and look into where it is that we're seeing data gaps.

Why are we even talking about giving credit to somebody? It's not a credit thing. It is "Can we track it or not?" And if we can't track it, and we have a hunch that it's actually working, then we have to start looking into other directional data that might be giving us hunches. For example, LinkedIn social selling. All the posts you have seen are not possible to track directly into, like, "Oh, I'm going to give the credit to LinkedIn for this one." You can't. But, in general, you know that some of the clients are speaking about those and we want to know those stories as well. So besides the Operations team's owning all the touches of the marketing and sales data and the data cleanness, there has to be some hunch about what is there beyond just what we can track. And should we ask our clients about that? Should we just look at our website traffic?

Let's say our team started to post on LinkedIn and after a month or two we can see that, "Oh, our MQLs are growing by 20% and we did nothing different, just that." Then you're able to see, okay, that's probably also working and let's continue doing that, and we can nurture that type of untrackable way as well. But the most important part—we don't give credit from one team to another. It is data. We pick it up from where the data is due, and it's tough. It's really, really hard. But as Operations, you have to make sure your website is properly tracked. You are mapping your campaigns. You've got your UTMs in place. Whenever somebody goes to events, they get them tracked. And for Sales to be able to contribute to that as well, they have to track their meetings, track their calls made. Whenever they meet people at events, they have to register them as well. So there is that cross-collaboration, and it's easier to look into the data to get those answers.

Chapter 16

Honesty in Reporting

In the scenario mentioned earlier, I stated that we, as members of the Sales and Marketing teams, can fall into the trap of reporting results and business deal narratives that simply are not true. This is less intentional than it is a result of siloed working environments, different KPIs, and, most critically, the reports that each team outputs. It's not uncommon for these departments to generate reports that are more aligned with their individual team's goals rather than the company's overall revenue objectives. This often-unintentional bias can lead to what might be considered "selfish" reporting.

When I give talks to business organizations on the CASH model, I often tell this story based on a classic humor piece:

Cash in a Casket

Once upon a time, a visionary founder built a successful company guided by strong principles and innovative ideas. As he neared the end of his life, he entrusted his three top executives—his CEO, CMO, and CFO—with a significant task. He gave each of them $100,000, asking that upon his passing they place the $300,000 in his casket as a symbolic gesture to uphold the company's values and his legacy.

When the founder sadly passed away, his wish was to be honored at his funeral. The CEO approached the casket first, placing an envelope inside and solemnly declaring that he had deposited $100,000 in cash, as requested. Following him, the CMO, equally somber, added another envelope with $100,000 in cash, affirming his adherence to their founder's final wish.

Last, the CFO calmly approached the casket. After looking around, he removed the two existing envelopes and pulled out his checkbook. He wrote a check for $300,000 and placed it inside the casket.

The CFO effectively upheld the founder's directive, right?

The CFO's action, though seemingly aligning with the numerical request, missed the essence of the founder's last wish. The numbers on the check were correct, but the true spirit of commitment and honesty was not met. He had not contributed the funds as explicitly intended, instead cleverly manipulating the situation to appear compliant without true sacrifice.

This story serves as a powerful analogy for what often transpires in our business reporting. Numbers can be made to align perfectly on reports, presenting an image of compliance and achievement. Yet, like the CFO's maneuver, if the underlying actions are not genuinely honest or aligned with the organization's core goals, then the true purpose is lost. Just as with the founder's last request, it isn't just the figures that matter. We have to consider the actual objectives and that they are honestly achieved. This emphasizes the need for integrity in all our professional dealings, ensuring that our actions reflect our words.

Now I'll illustrate how this fictional story plays out in real life and its implications.

Addressing the pitfalls of dishonest reporting stemming from team-specific goals and metrics is essential to building an effective Revenue team from distinct Sales and Marketing groups. Here's an expanded view, including illustrative examples, of how each scenario contributes to skewed reporting and how it can be mitigated through more aligned practices.

The Selective Highlighting of Metrics

Marketing teams might focus on metrics like website traffic, social media engagement, or email open rates, which, while indicative of audience interest, don't directly translate to sales or revenue. For instance, a marketing campaign might generate high engagement rates, but their business value remains questionable if these engagements do not convert into leads or sales.

Similarly, Sales teams might highlight the number of calls made or meetings held as a sign of productivity. However, without correlating these activities to actual sales outcomes or the quality of interactions, such metrics provide a limited view of effectiveness.

Impact on Honesty

By selectively highlighting favorable metrics, each team presents an overly optimistic view of their performance that doesn't necessarily align with overall business success. This selective reporting can mislead decision-makers about the actual state of business health and stall necessary strategic adjustments.

As a solution, organizations must implement a balanced scorecard approach that includes both leading (predictive) and lagging (outcome-based) indicators across teams. For instance, integrating marketing's lead generation numbers with sales conversion rates can provide a more comprehensive view of the customer acquisition process. Regular cross-functional reviews should be conducted to discuss these metrics, ensuring that all stakeholders have a clear and holistic view of organizational performance.

Overemphasis on Team-Specific Achievements

Which activities are truly effective? Is it trade shows, or is it business cards? Is it cold calls, or is it webinars? Is it wine and dine, or is it podcasts?

You won't know until you are open and honest about what activities discovered, nurtured, and drove your deals toward the signature line. (I should emphasize the word "toward" here. As we've explained before, one activity rarely works alone to close a deal.)

Marketing might report high numbers of content downloads or webinar attendees as a success without verifying if these initiatives attract the right prospects or lead to qualified leads. For example, a Marketing team could celebrate a record number of attendees at a promotional event. Still, if these attendees do not belong to the target demographic or fail to engage further with the company, the effort may not be beneficial in a business sense.

On the flip side, Sales might boast about the number of new accounts opened without acknowledging the overall profitability or lifetime value of these accounts. Salespeople might achieve their quota by focusing on more straightforward, low-value deals that don't significantly contribute to the company's revenue goals.

The honest impact is that when teams focus solely on metrics that reflect well on their efforts but don't necessarily positively impact the business, they create a distorted view of success. This misalignment can result in wasted resources and strategic misdirection.

A solution would be to create interconnected team objectives that require mutual contribution and accountability. For instance, Marketing should be tasked with not just generating leads that qualify for marketing (MQLs) but generating "sales-qualified leads" (SQLs). Likewise, Sales can be evaluated not only on the number of deals closed but also on the quality and value of those deals. Regular alignment sessions can help maintain focus on shared goals and adjust strategies as needed.

Misalignment of KPIs

Marketing's KPIs might include lead quantity without sufficient emphasis on lead quality. For example, they might celebrate generating thousands of leads from a campaign, but if these leads are not adequately qualified, the Sales team may waste time and resources pursuing unproductive prospects. This is especially true when measuring social media campaigns. While every effort should be measured and celebrated, we cannot lose sight (even if it requires years) of how these activities truly impact business.

Conversely, Sales might be focused solely on closing deals as quickly as possible to meet short-term goals, potentially neglecting longer-term strategies like nurturing high-value prospects who are not yet ready to buy but could provide substantial revenue in the future. This is common in organizations with long sales cycles and short measurement terms. This is a bad environment and scenario created by management and it can most easily be solved at that level.

The misalignment of KPIs encourages teams to report on metrics that make their performance appear effective but don't necessarily align with or contribute to the company's overarching objectives. It leads to inefficiencies and miscommunications between teams as they pursue divergent goals.

Again, this solution must start with management. Jointly develop and monitor KPIs that align with overarching business objectives. The sales cycle time frame must be considered in the overall measurement time frame of both the Sales and Marketing teams. When sales happen in halves and measurement is in quarters, you have created a recipe for disaster and a team that will bend the data to survive.

Introducing shared KPIs like funnel velocity, customer acquisition cost (CAC), and customer lifetime value (CLV) can help both teams focus on their individual contributions and their impact on the business's financial health as a whole. Regular strategy sessions to review these KPIs can encourage ongoing alignment and collaboration.

By tackling these issues head-on, organizations can foster a culture of honesty and accountability crucial for merging Sales and Marketing into a cohesive, effective Revenue team.

Expert Insight—Matt Crisp

Matt Crisp, introduced earlier, shares insight into the high quality of Sales, Marketing, and leadership alignment at eVestment Alliance during his time as the COO:

We sat down and said, "Here are the team goals. Here's how they roll up to the individual organizations at a functional level, and here's how they roll up at a company level." And we were open and honest about how all those work. So instead of creating an environment where Marketing says, "Look, I hit my goals. The company didn't hit its goals, but I hit mine. I want to get a bonus," we said, "Yes, there's a portion of your bonus tied to whether you hit your org goals, but a bigger portion is where the company hit its goal."

And so I think that level of honesty and transparency is what really helped us align—and people got on board, because they didn't feel like we were hiding. Like, "Well, you're asking us for all this data and to be honest with you about my leads and my pipeline, but you're not willing to share with us how that's rolling up at a company level. So if you're not willing to share, I'm not willing to share." We had to lead by example, and we did it early on. It didn't make sense not to communicate it. We really didn't have anything to hide.

Again, you get organizations that are doing some funky accounting stuff and they don't want a lot of people to know it. But for us, that integrity, that honesty and transparency— it made people buy in. Having a marketing person's bonus tied to the productivity of a salesperson was hard to do, but because they knew that, at a company level, everybody was aligned, we were ultimately able to get buy-in by at large. Now, you're going to get some people who don't, and those people end up not making it. They leave the company and go somewhere else.

We also had an option program; again, every single employee had options. Not just the key executive level, but every single employee after six months with the business was granted options. And that aligned everybody. And so Sales and Marketing worked with technology because they said, "You've got options. I've got options. If we write the right code and produce the right features and you sell the right features, we're all going to benefit!" So across the entire organization, but Sales and Marketing specifically, there was honesty and transparency and not feeling like, "Hey, look, you just give me leads and I'll go sell them. And you're not really that important to me anyway, because I'm the sales guy."

We minimized the amount of discontent that existed between those two organizations. But a lot of it was our leaders. They were amazing leaders, and they were willing to collaborate and truly tie their individual financial rewards to each other. And that's uncommon.

Chapter 17

Honesty in Goals

Communication and Honesty

Here I want to explore a scenario that could have just as well been in the Honesty in Reporting chapter; however, because of the impact on company goals and communication ethics, it deserves its own space.

One afternoon, upper management requested an in-depth report that required aggregating data from several systems. I managed data for our global division, but this request required data from corporate as well. The organization was big enough that a specific team was tasked with managing the marketing data at a corporate level.

I submitted a detailed request to the team that handled the corporate data, outlining the specifics needed for the report. They delivered the report by 5:30 pm. However, upon reviewing it, I discovered that the data analysts had incorporated incorrect data, which resulted in the report being inaccurate and misleading.

The manager of the team happened by my desk as he was leaving the office and I pointed this out to him. His response was nonchalant: "Look, man, they just want their report; nobody gives a sh** if it's *right or* *not—they just want a report."* I was shocked. I get that perfection is the enemy of done. I get that a lot of people had to cover their behinds and send reports up the ladder. I get that my manager wouldn't have known the difference anyway.

But the data was wrong, and I would be taking part in the fostering of dishonest reporting in an effort to satisfy my personal (and maybe my manager's) selfish goals.

In this scenario, there is a clear interaction between personal ethics, organizational culture, and managerial responsibility that highlights the fundamental need for honesty in business. Here's how each element plays a role:

At the center of this issue is the ethical dilemma I faced, reflecting deeper systemic problems within the organization. I was confronted with the challenge of whether to pass on incorrect data that could mislead decision-makers and damage the company's integrity. This conflict brings to light the ethical challenges employees might face when their job duties clash with their personal values.

The data manager's response to the data inaccuracies clearly shows a disregard for ethical standards and points to a larger organizational culture that prioritizes completing tasks over ensuring they are done correctly. This environment, where reports are submitted without careful verification, undermines trust and can lead to significant strategic mistakes based on incorrect information. It underscores how a lack of honesty can weaken the trust essential for a successful business operation.

The heart of the problem is exposed when my own manager casually dismisses the data inaccuracies. This behavior reveals a significant issue in our leadership's commitment to integrity and data accuracy. By choosing speed over thoroughness, the data manager and his team undermine diligent employees' efforts and reduce our organizational processes' reliability.

These points strongly support the need to cultivate a culture that values honesty and integrity, starting with leadership and extending to every team member. It's crucial for fostering an environment where ethical behavior is standard practice and the accuracy of information is upheld. This approach is vital for maintaining stakeholder trust and ensuring the business's long-term success.

Alignment and Honesty

In this book, we've touched on several areas where alignment affected honesty. When Oren, the VP of Sales, aligned with Marketing to save his trade show participation, it showed the company that Sales wasn't successful alone. That honesty led to data conversations, allowing him to prove the value of attendance at the expensive trade show.

When the inside salesperson hoarded data, the result was dishonest reporting. This resulted in misaligned efforts with both the Sales executives and Marketing efforts. When Marketing or Sales reporting is department-centered rather than aligned as a Revenue team supporting the organization, the result is a dishonest depiction of success.

Alignment involves setting and agreeing on realistic goals that reflect the true objectives of both Sales and Marketing. It's about establishing a mutual understanding of what success looks like, supported by metrics that resonate across both teams. Honest alignment ensures that both teams are accountable to each other and share a commitment to common goals.

For instance, if the shared objective is to enhance penetration in a specific market segment, Marketing needs to tailor campaigns to generate relevant awareness, while Sales should follow up with targeted outreach. This honest agreement on strategies and outcomes ensures that resources are effectively utilized, driving toward shared business objectives.

Systems and Honesty

The systems we use can be one of the best tools to support honesty between Sales and Marketing. The data doesn't lie (if reported correctly). Data-driven decisions drive honesty as long as we encourage both teams to participate in collecting and reporting the data. CRM tools and marketing automation platforms provide comprehensive views of the customer journey, allowing both teams to base their strategies on solid, actionable insights rather than assumptions.

For instance, CRM systems show Sales that Marketing's efforts have effectively engaged customers, enabling them to fine-tune their approach accordingly. Similarly, Marketing can identify which strategies lead to actual sales conversions and adjust their campaigns to optimize results.

This continuous exchange of information enhances each team's effectiveness and highlights how their activities are interlinked, directly impacting each other's success. For example, detailed lead scoring from Marketing can significantly increase the efficiency of Sales follow-ups, demonstrating the dependency of Sales on Marketing's accuracy. By documenting the outcomes of specific strategies, these systems hold each team accountable, allowing for quick recalibration of tactics that aren't performing well.

Regular data analysis from these systems helps predict customer behavior and market trends, enabling Sales and Marketing to adjust their strategies proactively. This keeps both teams agile and ensures they are consistently aligned with the overall business objectives.

Using these systems helps Sales and Marketing stay transparent and collaborative, which leads to better decisions and ongoing success.

Surfacing the Revenue Team

In this book we have discussed a framework and its values that will transform how your Sales and Marketing teams operate. This book provides a blueprint for merging these teams into a single, powerful revenue machine, rather than having them function as separate entities. The essence of CASH revolves around four key themes: Communication, Alignment, Systems, and Honesty. Each plays a critical role in bridging the gap between Sales and Marketing, ensuring they work in harmony rather than isolation.

We began by emphasizing the crucial role of effective communication, detailing how open and continuous exchanges between teams enhance understanding and collaboration. Next, we discussed the importance of alignment, where a mutual understanding of roles crystallizes how each team's efforts complement the other, driving toward shared goals. Our discussion on systems highlighted the integration of technology and processes as a backbone for strategic decisions, enhancing the efficiency of collaborative efforts. Finally, we underscored the value of honesty in fostering a trust-rich environment that celebrates transparency and accountability.

As you look to strengthen your understanding of Sales and Marketing, envision your organization as one with effective Sales and Marketing teams designed as a cohesive unit—a revenue machine powered by the principles of CASH. Implementing this framework will streamline your operations while cultivating a workplace where shared successes are the cornerstone of your corporate culture.

To further this growth, I encourage you to subscribe to our newsletter at ALeeJudge.com. Here you'll gain access to ongoing insights and resources that support the continuous improvement of sales and marketing cohesion. Additionally, connect with me on LinkedIn to stay engaged with our growing community of professionals dedicated to this cause.

For organizations ready to learn more deeply, we offer the CASH workshop—a tailored experience designed to apply the CASH principles directly to your team dynamics and challenges. Reach out through ALeeJudge.com to invite me and my team to facilitate this paradigm-shifting workshop. Together, we can turn the theoretical into the practical, significantly impacting your organization's success.

This book is your starting point; the journey toward unified Sales and Marketing is ongoing. With each step, you'll discover that the true strength of your business lies in its ability to adapt, integrate, and celebrate the collective efforts of your teams. Join us in this movement and redefine what it means to succeed in today's dynamic business environment.

— A. LEE JUDGE

About the Author

A. Lee Judge is a distinguished authority in the fields of Sales and Marketing, recognized for his deep expertise and innovative approaches to bridging the gap between these two critical business functions. With over 20 years of experience, Lee has made significant contributions to the industry, helping organizations harmonize their sales and marketing efforts to drive cohesive revenue growth.

Professional Background

Lee's career is a testament to his versatile skills and strategic vision. As a digital marketing leader, he has developed a unique ability to speak the languages of sales, marketing, and customer experience, making him a sought-after consultant and keynote speaker. His hands-on technical acumen and executive-level marketing experience allow him to offer unparalleled insights into the alignment of business processes, sales operations, and marketing strategies.

Key Contributions

Consulting and Training

Lee has been instrumental in providing strategic advice and training to businesses seeking to optimize their digital marketing and sales processes. His expertise spans marketing automation, CRM integration, content marketing, and sales enablement. Through his consulting services, Lee helps organizations develop and execute holistic marketing strategies that enhance their overall selling capabilities and improve execution and conversion rates.

Content Entrepreneur

As the cofounder and Chief Marketing Officer of Content Monsta, a content marketing agency, Lee has pioneered innovative content strategies that leverage multimedia to maximize ROI. His work in creating engaging videos, podcasts, and emerging digital content has helped numerous brands elevate their digital presence and attract more inbound traffic.

Speaking and Thought Leadership

Lee's dynamic speaking style and ability to engage audiences have made him a popular keynote speaker at major industry events. His presentations are known for being informative, motivational, and thought-provoking, covering key topics such as Sales and Marketing alignment, content marketing, and content production for business. Lee's sessions are highly praised for their practical insights and actionable takeaways, leaving attendees equipped with the knowledge and motivation to implement positive changes in their organizations.

Vision and Philosophy

Lee's approach to marketing is centered on understanding the customer journey and aligning the efforts of Sales and Marketing to meet business objectives. He advocates for a data-driven and customer-centric strategy, emphasizing the importance of creating meaningful connections with audiences through engaging content and strategic communication.

Through speaking appearances, this book, and entrepreneurial endeavors, A. Lee Judge continues to inspire and guide business leaders toward achieving greater cohesion and success in their sales and marketing initiatives. His expertise and passion for the field make him a pivotal figure in the ongoing evolution of digital marketing and sales strategies.

Glossary of Sales and Marketing Terms

A

A/B Testing: A method of comparing two versions of an asset (such as an email, web page, or other content) to determine which performs better. The goal is to see which version, Version A or Version B, wins.

Account-Based Marketing (ABM): A strategic approach focusing on creating personalized campaigns for specific high-value accounts rather than targeting a broader audience.

Ad Retargeting: A form of online advertising that targets users who have previously visited your website with specific ads or taken a trackable action as they browse other sites.

Affiliate Marketing: A performance-based marketing strategy where businesses reward affiliates (partners) for each visitor or customer brought by the affiliate's marketing efforts.

AIDA Model: A marketing framework outlining the stages a consumer goes through when making a purchase: attention, interest, desire, and action.

Alignment: The strategic coordination between teams to ensure they work toward common goals, such as increasing revenue and improving customer engagement. This involves clear communication, shared metrics, and collaborative planning, enabling both teams to support each other effectively from lead generation to closing sales. By aligning their activities, Sales and Marketing can reduce friction, improve efficiency, and provide a seamless customer experience.

Analytics: The discovery and interpretation of meaningful patterns in data, often used to measure performance and inform business decisions. Artificial Intelligence (AI): The development of computer systems and algorithms that can perform tasks typically requiring human intelligence. These tasks include understanding natural language, recognizing patterns, solving problems, learning from experience, and making decisions.

Attribution Modeling: The process of determining which touchpoints are responsible for driving conversions and assigning value to each one.

B
—

B2B (Business-to-Business): Commercial transactions or relationships between two businesses rather than between a business and individual consumers.

B2C (Business-to-Consumer): Transactions or relationships between a business and individual consumers.

Big Data: Extremely large data sets that can be analyzed computationally to reveal patterns, trends, and associations, especially relating to human behavior and interactions.

Bottom of the Funnel (BOFU): The final stage in the buying process where leads are close to making a purchase decision.

Brand Advocacy: Customers who proactively promote a brand or product, often through word of mouth, social media, or other channels.

Brand Awareness: The extent to which consumers recognize and are familiar with a brand, often seen as the first step in the customer journey.

Brand Equity: The value that a brand adds to a product, as perceived by consumers, based on the brand's strength in the market.

Brand Loyalty: A customer's commitment to repurchase or continue using a brand, often demonstrated by repeat purchases and positive word of mouth.

Buyer Persona: A detailed profile that represents a business's ideal customer, based on market research and real data about existing customers.

Buying Center: A group of individuals within an organization responsible for making purchasing decisions.

C
—

Churn Rate: The percentage of customers who stop doing business with a company over a given period.

Click-through Rate (CTR): The percentage of users who click on a specific link compared with the total number of users who view a page, email, or advertisement.

Content Curation: The process of gathering, organizing, and sharing high-quality content on a particular topic from various sources.

Content Marketing: A strategy focused on creating and distributing valuable, relevant, and consistent content to attract and retain a target audience.

Conversion Funnel: A model describing the stages a potential customer goes through to become a buyer, emphasizing conversion points along the journey.

Conversion Rate: The percentage of users who take a desired action, such as making a purchase or signing up for a newsletter. Marketing conversions represent a person going from unknown to known. Sales conversions indicate a prospect has become a customer.

Conversion Rate Optimization (CRO): The systematic process of increasing the percentage of website visitors who take a desired action.

Cost per Acquisition (CPA): The cost of acquiring a new customer or lead, calculated by dividing the total cost of marketing by the number of new customers acquired.

Cost per Click (CPC): The amount paid by an advertiser for each click on its advertisement.

Cost per Impression (CPM): The cost of an advertisement per 1,000 impressions or views.

Cost per Lead (CPL): A metric that measures the cost-effectiveness of generating a lead, calculated by dividing the total cost of a marketing campaign by the number of leads generated.

Customer Acquisition Cost (CAC): The cost associated with acquiring a new customer, including marketing and sales expenses.

Customer Experience (CX): The overall perception and feelings a customer has about their interactions with a business, from initial contact through the entire customer life cycle.

Customer Life Cycle: The entire journey a customer takes from initial awareness through purchase and beyond, including retention and loyalty.

Customer Lifetime Value (CLTV): The total net profit a company can expect to earn from a customer throughout a business relationship.

Customer Relationship Management (CRM): Refers to both the technology and strategy used to manage a company's interactions with current and potential customers, often via software platforms like Salesforce, Hubspot, and Zoho.

Customer Segmentation: Dividing a customer base into groups based on shared characteristics, behaviors, or needs in order to tailor marketing efforts effectively.

Customer Success: A proactive approach to helping customers achieve their desired outcomes while using a company's product or service, often leading to higher retention and satisfaction.

D

Data-Driven Marketing: The practice of optimizing brand communications based on customer information and data insights.

Demand Generation: Marketing strategies focused on creating awareness and interest in a company's products or services.

Digital Marketing: The use of digital channels and technologies to promote or market products and services to consumers and businesses.

Digital Transformation: The integration of digital technology into all areas of a business, fundamentally changing how the company operates and delivers value to customers.

Direct Marketing: A type of advertising that allows businesses to communicate directly with customers through a variety of media including email, text messaging, and postal mail.

E

Email Marketing: A digital marketing strategy that uses email to communicate value, educate customers, send advertisements, request business, or solicit sales and donations.

Engagement Rate: A metric that measures the level of interaction consumers have with content, such as likes, shares, comments, and other actions.

G

Go-to-Market Strategy: A plan that outlines how a company will reach target customers and achieve competitive advantage in the marketplace.

I

Ideal Customer Profile (ICP): A detailed description of a company's perfect customer, based on various attributes such as demographics (industry, company size, revenue, location) or psychographics (attitudes, aspirations, lifestyle, interests, and other psychological criteria). An ICP helps businesses identify and focus their marketing and sales efforts on the most valuable potential customers, leading to more efficient targeting and better conversion rates.

Inbound Marketing: A strategy focused on attracting customers through relevant and helpful content rather than interruptive advertising.

Influencer Marketing: A form of social media marketing involving endorsements and product placements from influencers, individuals, and organizations with a purported expert level of knowledge or social influence.

Integrated Marketing Communications (IMC): The coordination and integration of all marketing communication tools, avenues, and sources within a company into a seamless program designed to maximize the impact on consumers and other end users at a minimal cost.

K

Key Account Management (KAM): A strategic approach to managing and nurturing a company's most important accounts to maximize mutual value.

Key Performance Indicators (KPIs): Metrics used to assess the performance of various business activities and ensure alignment with strategic goals.

L
—

Landing Page: A stand-alone web page created specifically for a marketing or advertising campaign, designed to capture leads or drive conversions.

Lead: A potential customer who has shown interest in a company's product or service and may eventually become a buyer.

Lead Conversion Rate: The percentage of leads that convert into customers, indicating the effectiveness of both marketing and sales efforts.

Lead Generation: The process of attracting and converting strangers and prospects into potential customers who have indicated interest in a company's product or service.

Lead Management: The process of tracking and managing potential customers (leads) through the sales funnel to increase the likelihood of conversion.

Lead Nurturing: The process of developing relationships with buyers at every stage of the sales funnel and through every step of the buyer's journey.

Lead Scoring: A methodology used to rank prospects against a scale that represents the perceived value each lead represents to the organization.

Lee's Ps: A modern framework that emphasizes the importance of presence, perception, pricing, and profitability in the marketing strategy, reflecting the evolving dynamics between Sales and Marketing in achieving business success. Lee's Ps leaves out the traditional marketing mix items of product, place, and promotion because the focus is on strategic concepts like presence, perception, and profitability that influence consumer behavior and market dynamics in a digital and global context.

Look-Alike Audience: A type of audience created by identifying common qualities of a company's existing customers and finding new potential customers who share those qualities.

M
—

Market Penetration: A strategy used to increase the market share of an existing product or service in existing markets, often through competitive pricing, marketing, and promotions.

Market Research: The process of gathering, analyzing, and interpreting information about a market, including information about the target market, customers, competitors, and industry.

Market Segmentation: The practice of dividing a target market into smaller, more defined categories based on various characteristics, such as demographics or behavior.

Marketing Automation Platforms (MAPs): Software tools that automate marketing activities, such as email marketing, social media posting, ad campaigns, and lead scoring.

Marketing Qualified Leads (MQLs): Prospects who have shown enough interest to be considered more likely to become customers compared with other leads, based on marketing efforts.

Marketing ROI: The measurement of the profit or loss generated by marketing activities, relative to the amount of money invested.

Marketing Strategy: The overall game plan for reaching prospective consumers and turning them into customers of the products or services the business provides.

Middle of the Funnel (MOFU): The middle stage in the buying process, where leads have shown interest and are considering doing business with a company.

Multichannel Marketing: A marketing strategy that uses multiple channels to reach customers, such as email, social media, websites, and retail outlets.

N

Net Promoter Score (NPS): A customer loyalty and satisfaction measurement taken by asking customers how likely they are to recommend your product or service to others.

Niche Marketing: Targeting a specific, defined segment of the market that is often underserved by larger competitors.

O

Omnichannel Marketing: A cross-channel content strategy that organizations use to improve their user experience and drive better relationships across all points of contact.

Outbound Marketing: Traditional marketing methods focused on reaching out to potential customers, such as TV ads, print media, telemarketing, and trade shows. This is a direct contrast to inbound marketing.

P

Pay per Click (PPC): An internet advertising model used to drive traffic to websites, where an advertiser pays a publisher when the ad is clicked.

Pipeline Management: The process of overseeing and directing future sales in various stages of the purchasing process.

Positioning: The act of designing the company's offering and image to occupy a distinct place in the minds of the target market.

Predictive Analytics: The use of data, statistical algorithms, and machine learning techniques to identify the likelihood of future outcomes based on historical data.

Product Life Cycle: The stages a product goes through from development to introduction to the market to growth, maturity, and decline.

Public Relations (PR): The strategic communication process that builds mutually beneficial relationships between organizations and their public.

R
——

Referral Marketing: A method of promoting products or services to new customers through referrals, usually word of mouth.

Revenue Funnel: A unified model of sales and marketing that aligns efforts and strategies to guide prospects through the buying process and convert them into customers.

S
——

Sales Enablement: The process of providing Sales teams with the information, content, and tools they need to sell effectively.

Sales Funnel: The process through which potential customers are guided from initial awareness to a final purchase, often visualized as a funnel with stages like awareness, interest, decision, and action.

Sales Pipeline: A visual representation of sales prospects and where they are in the purchasing process.

Sales Qualified Leads (SQLs): Leads that have been vetted further by Sales teams after initial qualification by Marketing and are considered ready for a deeper sales conversation.

Search Engine Optimization (SEO): The process of improving the visibility of a website or web page in a search engine's unpaid results.

Segmentation: Dividing a broad consumer or business market into subgroups of consumers based on shared characteristics.

Social Media Marketing (SMM): The use of social media platforms and websites to promote a product or service.

T
——

Target Market: A specific group of consumers at which a company aims its products and services.

Targeting: The process of selecting specific segments to focus marketing efforts on based on the segment's attractiveness and fit with the company's objectives.

Top of the Funnel (TOFU): The initial stage of the buying process, where potential customers become aware of a product or service.

Touchpoint: Any interaction between a customer and a business, from prepurchase to postpurchase, that influences the customer's perception of the brand.

U

Unique Selling Proposition (USP):
A factor that differentiates a product from its competitors, such as the lowest cost, highest quality, or a unique feature.

User-Generated Content (UGC):
Any content, such as text, videos, images, or reviews, created by consumers about a brand or product, often shared on social media or other platforms.

V

Value Proposition: A statement that explains how a product solves a problem, delivers specific benefits, and tells the ideal customer why they should buy from you and not from the competition.

W

Webinar: A live or recorded online presentation or workshop that is transmitted over the internet.

Word of Mouth (WOM): The passing of information from person to person by oral communication, which plays a crucial role in influencing customer decisions.